WRITERS ON WRITING

CONVERSATIONS WITH ALLEN MENDENHALL

Critical Praise for Writers on Writing: Conversations with Allen Mendenhall

"Anyone interested in the lives of present-day American writers, and particularly of writers who come from the South or take the South as their subject, will find the interviews compiled in Allen Mendenhall's *Writers on Writing* an unalloyed pleasure. Mendenhall is the most gentle and conversational of interviewers, and his book consists of interview after interview with writers, famous and obscure alike, who are pleased to talk freely about their writing habits, their careers, and their ambitions. The result is a book that manages to be a serious romp, full of insight and full of fun."

-**Wilfred M. McClay,** G.T. and Libby Blankenship Chair in the History of Liberty, University of Oklahoma

"A better way to put John Gardner's famous quote might be 'Writing is the only religion I have.' The writers in this anthology demonstrate this kind of passion, intellectual curiosity, and devotion to the world of ideas, and all the ways in which a writer reorganizes a life to pursue a life in writing. This anthology of interviews gives the reader insight into how a writer thinks, whether it's writing fiction, poetry, or pursuing academic work. These interviews are inspiring, engaging, and ought to be required reading for anyone who loves the written word."

-**Daren Dean,** Department of English, Louisiana State University, author of *Far Beyond the Pale*

"The interviews in *Writers on Writing* are not formulaic Q&As, but organic conversations with a diverse group of writers, including numerous award-winning and *New York Times* best-selling authors. Mendenhall shows us more than the art and craft of these writers—a group that includes novelists, historians, memoirists, social commentators, essayists, poets, and writers of mystery, legal and crime thrillers, and literary criticism. He reveals their hearts."

-**Susan Cushman,** Editor of *Southern Writers on Writing* and *A Second Blooming: Becoming the Women We Are Meant to Be,* author of the novel *Cherry Bomb* and the memoir *Tangles and Plaques: A Mother and Daughter Face Alzheimer's*

"This collection of writers on writing contains smart, perceptive interviews with diverse authors and offers unique and fascinating insights into the creative mind and processes. Each interview unearths delicious and precious nuggets that are as captivating as they are revelatory."

-**Nancy Dillingham,** author of the poetry collections *New Ground, Home,* and *Like Headlines*

"*Writers on Writing* takes us on a delightful stroll through recent Southern literature, with Allen Mendenhall as our expert guide. A polymath who wears his learning well, Mendenhall poses questions both inviting and incisive. He encourages authors to take him—and therefore, us—into their confidence, providing valuable insights into dozens of books and the sensibilities that brought them into being."

-**Gilbert Allen,** Professor Emeritus, Furman University, Department of English

Writers on Writing: Conversations with Allen Mendenhall ©2019
All rights reserved. In accordance with the U.S. Copyright Act of 1976, the scanning, uploading, and electronic sharing of any part of this book without the permission of the publisher is unlawful piracy and theft of the author's intellectual property. If you would like to use material from the book (other than for review purposes), written permission must be obtained by contacting the publisher at reddirtpress@yahoo.com (www.reddirtpress.net). Thank you for your support of the author's rights.

Cover and Interior Design: Greg Gilpin, Graphic Art Center, Inc.
Cover Art: Greg Gilpin, Graphic Art Center, Inc.
www.graphicartcenter.com

Red Dirt Press
1831 N. Park Ave.
Shawnee, OK 74804
www.reddirtpress.net

ISBN: 978-1-7327383-2-4

Table of Contents

Foreword 9
Introduction 11
Interviews
    F.H. Buckley.. 13
    Shuly Cawood 17
    Robert P. Waxler 23
    Johnnie Bernhard 31
    Steve Wiegenstein 35
    Dan Leach 41
    DJ Donaldson 47
    Kelly Kennington 51
    Lorna Hollifield 55
    Idabel Allen 59
    Emily Carpenter 63
    Jessica Hooten Wilson 67
    Amber D. Tran 71
    Katherine Clark 75
    Bren McClain 79
    Danny Johnson 83
    Julia Nunnally Duncan (first interview) 87
    Deborah Mantella 91

Derek Furr 95
Glenn Arbery 99
Russell Scott 105
Elizabeth Harris 107
Lindsay Parnell 113
Hubert Crouch 121
M. Maitland Deland 125
Howard G. Franklin 129
Stephen Roth 137
Paul A. Cantor 141
Tom Turner 147
F. Diane Pickett 151
Colleen D. Scott 155
David Joy 159
Mark Schimmoeller 165

Richelle Putnam	169
Robert J. Ernst	173
Barbara Davis	177
Jolina Petersheim	181
Jeff High	185
David Bradley	191
Jessica Dotta	199
Karen White	205
Lauren Clark	209
Julia Nunnally Duncan (second interview)	211
Coleman Hutchison	213
Jeffrey Tucker	219
John Shelton Reed	223
William Bernhardt	227
Acknowledgments	229

Foreword

Some words become so familiar to us, so early, that we don't think much about them *as* words. Some derive in interesting ways from other languages: how many people know that the word "conversation" derives from a Latin verb meaning "to turn about"? To learn that origin is to gain a new understanding of what conversation is: people turning to one another, and being turned *by* one another, in a reciprocal sharing of perspective.

We don't have to look to other languages for such enlightenment, though: sometimes we just need to pay proper attention to our own vocabulary. For instance, everyone learns early on that "discover" means something like "find" or "realize." A student discovers Flannery O'Connor's *Complete Stories* in her school library and reads it cover to cover; that experience leads her to try her own hand at writing fiction, and she discovers that she enjoys it and is good at it. Think about the word's construction, how it combines the negative prefix "dis-" with "cover." Once you register that assembly, the word becomes wonderfully metaphorical. (As Ralph Waldo Emerson says, "Language is fossil poetry.") In discovering that book, our student removes it from its hiding place on a library shelf; in discovering her own gift, she has in a sense unhidden it from herself.

Consider one more word: "interview." We all know what it means, but when we use it, do we really notice what it's made of? "Inter-" + "view" = a meeting between people so they can look at each other, take each other in. That suggests more of a two-way affair than the word generally evokes, not so much interrogation as conversation—in other words, person A and person B turning toward each other.

The interviews collected here reflect that sense of mutuality. Not that Allen Mendenhall himself ever becomes their subject, but repeatedly we find two people having genuine exchanges—for the benefit of any who might enjoy and learn from them later. Mendenhall's friendship with some of these authors enlivens those interviews to a special degree, but here also are first encounters that result in reflective, valuable dialogue. This isn't simply a book of responses to questionnaires. In his classic study *I and Thou,* Martin Buber declares, "Alles wirkliche Leben ist Begegnung" ("All real life is encounter"); this is a book of real life.

Another remarkable aspect of *Writers on Writing* is its catholicity. Here are interviews centering on recent novels, short story collections, poetry volumes, historical studies, and literary studies. Some of those books are published by well-known commercial houses, some by university presses, some by small independent presses, and a few by the authors themselves. There's a delightful egalitarianism here, one that sets this book apart from other interview collections and makes its sweeping title all the more appropriate. It's not a book of fiction writers on writing, it's not a book of historians on writing, and it's not a book of poets or literary scholars on writing. It doesn't focus on best-selling authors or critical darlings. It's a book of thoughtful writers on writing, interviewed by another thoughtful writer. Come listen to the conversation; you'll make many happy discoveries.

Robert West
Starkville, Miss.
September 5, 2018

Introduction

I've been drawn to interviews with writers and creatives for as long as I can remember. I enjoy browsing the interview archives of *The Paris Review* and have learned from them that there's no right way to ask questions: You just follow your curiosities and hope your interlocutor is open and honest.

People respond differently to probing inquiry: some grow defensive, some coy; some wax poetic; some provide long, forthcoming responses while others clam up. We all have idiosyncrasies and unique personalities, which interviews are meant to uncover or air.

The following book consists of my interviews with several writers. For the most part, I have simply reproduced them as they originally appeared in various publications. I have, however, taken the liberty of removing underlined hyperlinks that were visible in the online versions of these interviews, and have removed *pro forma* questions and responses about where an author's book can be purchased. Every serious reader knows that books can be purchased online in less than a minute, usually from multiple booksellers. Besides, some of the links and purchasing sources are now outdated.

In some places I have separated one long paragraph into shorter, multiple paragraphs to ease the reading experience, and have corrected unfortunate misspellings that happened to appear in the original text.

My impulse was to add updated biographical entries for each interviewee, but I decided against it. When these interviews originally appeared, the interviewees, most of them anyway, supplied their preferred biographical narrative. Writers can be finicky and fussy. I didn't want to delay publication of this book while they fretted over their latest personal profile. So I didn't ask anyone for updated biographies. Suffice it to say, if you're interested in a particular interview and haven't heard of the writer before, search for him or her online. You'll find biographical details and more.

There's not much else to say. I'll let the writers do the talking and leave their words to your judgment.

—APM

F.H. Buckley

AM: Thanks for doing this interview, Frank. Your last book, *The Way Back*, addressed issues of economic inequality and the rise of the New Class, a manifestation of an old form of aristocracy consisting of people who can, so to speak, "game the system" through special favors and loopholes in laws. Your new book, *The Republic of Virtue*, is an extension of that theme, focusing on government corruption. It's come to light that the Justice Department is investigating activities of the Clinton Foundation, a target of yours. What does this investigation mean for our "Machiavellian moment," a term you use in the book?

FHB: Thanks for having me, Allen! The new book, *The Republic of Virtue*, is a companion to my 2016 book, *The Way Back* (now out in paperback). The earlier book described a crisis in American politics, the demise of the American Dream of a mobile society in which our children would have it better than we did. *The Republic of Virtue* details how we got here, through a deformed political system in which our politics are dominated by the greatest network of patronage and influence ever seen in the world.

That's not what the Framers of our Constitution wanted. They admired British liberty, but not British corruption, and the constitution they gave us was meant as an anti-corruption covenant. They had read their Plutarch and like Machiavelli yearned for disinterested leaders who would seek to serve the public interest. Hence the term, "Machiavellian Moment." We had another Machiavellian Moment in 2016, when voters saw in Hillary Clinton the very personification of corruption.

AM: What did corruption mean for our Framers?

FHB: Corruption meant Britain, the way votes were purchased on the hustings or in Parliament. It meant putting self-interest over the public good. They had a strong sense of fallen humanity, George Washington, James Madison, Gouverneur Morris, all of them. But they hoped they had found an answer to private vices in a Constitution that promoted public virtue. For some, this meant a strong national government, since they thought that self-interested leaders were more likely to be found at the state level. For others it meant just the opposite—strong state governments that would be closer to the people. With Gouverneur Morris and James Madison, some thought that the parts of the federal government should be kept distinct, in a separation of powers, to prevent coalition-building and "cabals." In the end they were not entirely sure what they had given us, except that all thought we needed to unite over a constitution, and all hoped that it would give us a set of disinterested leaders such as the man on the dais before them—George Washington.

AM: Their hopes have not materialized, I'm afraid. It takes more than a constitution to thwart corruption, doesn't it?

FHB: There are a good many myths about the framing of the Constitution that the Framers necessarily had to come to an agreement, that it was a "Madisonian" document. But the greatest myth was perhaps that of a machine that would run by itself. Relative to parliamentary government, in Walter Bagehot's day eighty years later, presidential government fairly welcomed corruption.

AM: Your book seamlessly weaves accounts of recent corruption scandals with more distant historical antecedents.

FHB: The Framers saw corruption at first hand when some of them visited Britain. They also saw it in the low mean politics of Albany and Orange County VA. But nothing could have prepared them for today's Washington. And there's a simple reason for that. There is, amongst governments in the world, no greater concentration of wealth than in Washington. At the same time, thanks to technological changes, it is easier to assemble an interest group at the national level than Madison could ever have imagined. Hence the crony capitalism of the K Street lobbyists.

It is fashionable today to blame the "deep state," the regulatory apparatus, for all this. Don't believe it. There's a regulatory state in every country. The difference is that we're richer than other countries, and there's more boodle to capture here.

AM: You mentioned that this book is a companion to *The Way Back*. What drew you to these subjects? Are they a long-standing academic interest of yours or were you compelled to write about them in light of political circumstances? Perhaps both?

FHB: If 2016 was a Machiavellian moment, it was also a Hamiltonian moment. In this, I am referring to W.D. Hamilton, the evolutionary biologist, who was possibly the greatest 20th century conservative. Hamilton proposed the "gene's eye" view of human action, which Richard Dawkins later called the "selfish gene" hypothesis. In *The Way Back* I explain that this is why we are impelled to favor our descendants over ourselves. And that explains 2016, where ordinary Americans recognized that the American Dream, the idea that our children would have it better than we did, was broken. The Republican Establishment missed this, of course. Against stupidity, the gods themselves are helpless, said Schiller. And he hadn't even met a Republican!

AM: I thought your discussions of evolutionary biology in *The Way Back* were fascinating. Equally fascinating is the regression analysis employed at the end of your book. What is regression analysis, and why did you use it?

FHB: Regression analysis is a statistical technique to isolate the contribution of different factors in explaining their correlation with a predicted variable. What I was able to show is that presidential regimes generally are less free and more corrupt than parliamentary governments. In short, to the extent that America is free and virtuous, that's in spite of and not because of its constitution. America is free because it's American, and not because the Framers gave us a perfect constitution in 1787.

AM: You've tackled several subjects in *The Republic of Virtue*, including corruption, republicanism, the Constitution, the separation-of-powers doctrine, federalism, and more. You've even proposed some reforms. How optimistic are you that we'll find our "way back," to borrow your coined phrase?

FHB: The title of the book, *Republic of Virtue*, is ironic. There is no republic of virtue, and people who thought they could get there found, like Robespierre, that a few heads had to be chopped off in the process. Instead of grand reforms, therefore, we should concentrate on the smaller reforms that I propose, which are principally directed at curbing the influence of lobbyists. We cannot and would not want to prevent them from offering information to elected officials. But at the same time there is no reason why they should be permitted to contribute and help organize Congressional campaigns, or worse still offer jobs to Congressmen.

AM: Thanks again for the interview.

Shuly Cawood

AM: Shuly, thanks for this interview about your memoir, *The Going and Goodbye*. **I want to start by asking you about the epigraph by Richard Wilbur, in part because he passed away just about the time your book was released. I find that intriguing because you quote him on the subject of life and death, which you grapple with in the book.**

SC: I was lucky enough to meet Richard Wilbur when he came to my undergraduate university not long after he had served as poet laureate. Because I was one of the editors of the literary magazine, I had the privilege of having lunch and spending some hours with him, along with other students. A few years later, while in graduate school for journalism, I took some poetry writing classes as a way to get through my journalism degree (not that the journalism program was bad—I just longed to be studying creative writing). In one poetry class, my professor, David Citino, asked that we all memorize and recite a poem, and I chose "The Writer," which is where the epigraph comes from. To this day, I cherish the poem for what it did for me then—help propel me through a master's degree I didn't love but that served me well—but also for the story the poem tells: of someone needing to write in order to, in essence, live.

AM: Could you live without writing?

SC: Yes, but I think I would suffer now without writing. It has helped me grapple with and understand a great many things in life, and it has served as a steady companion. That being said, I can imagine that it's possible that one day I won't turn to it anymore. I journaled from when I was a child until about ten years ago—journaling was a constant in my life. One day I just stopped for no apparent reason, and I haven't journaled since. I think things can run their course.

AM: As I read your book, I felt a tugging, aching longing for people and places of my past, even as the story was yours. With every gain in life, it seems, there's a corresponding loss, just as there's a loss with every gain. Most of these involve relationships, romantic or otherwise, and the remarkable way in which our emotional state at any given moment is bound up in the feelings and desires of others.

SC: One of the things I wrote in the book was that I like beginnings, before I've had to pick one thing over another—because with every decision, there is one thing that gets chosen and another that isn't, sometimes many others. And those others have always been hard for me—I am capable of grieving deeply for them. It's taken me a long time to realize that those choices might not have turned out as I used to imagine them. What's that saying? Something about how unhappiness comes from focusing on what isn't rather than what is. I believe that.

AM: I realize that writers of memoirs and personal essays always get asked about this, but I'm curious nonetheless. Do you feel any misgivings or hesitation when you write about those who are close to you, or have been close to you? I'm thinking, for instance, of Rob or Matthew or Preston.

SC: I wish that I didn't have to tell any of their stories in order to tell mine, but all the people in my book played a significant role in my life's journey. I tried to only tell the stories of theirs that I thought were necessary. I did my best to examine my own actions and behavior as much if not more than I did theirs. That's the job of a memoirist. Perhaps most importantly, I tried to be fair, but let's face it: it's inherently unfair that I'm the judge of what's fair. Still, I hope that if they were to read the book, they would think it was fair. I read my book over and over trying to see it from their point of view. In the end, I knew I had done my very best to be both honest and fair. Whether I achieved that, I cannot say.

AM: Why do you write creative nonfiction? To work through problems, feelings, and emotions? To study yourself? To vent? To entertain?

SC: I think it all depends on the piece—the reason or reasons can change. I write some things to share a story with someone, or to entertain; other things I write and don't know why I am writing it, or I figure it out along the way. As for my memoir in particular, I wrote it to make sense of parts of my life—to understand why I had made the life choices I had made. Along the way, I ended up learning more about the people in my life and how they might have felt, how I might have affected them, failed them.

AM: Do you think your closeness to the funeral business makes you more attentive or sensitive as a writer?

SC: I don't know that it's changed my writing. It's changed my life, though. I've always been sensitive, but it's helped me understand grief better and how people handle it in such different ways. And I've certainly learned what it means to have a good funeral.

I've also learned a lot about my husband as I witness how he shapes his business to help people as they take their journey through grief. He's taught me a great deal about generosity, too, and commitment to giving back to and improving the community.

AM: Could you talk about the importance of memory? Your book is attentive to the possibility that you haven't recalled some things fully—that there are details you might have forgotten. Joyce Dyer is quoted on the cover of your book as saying, "This is a voice you can trust with your life." I find that interesting given that you work professionally with death, but also because, in my view, your honesty about memory—its limitations, refractions, and blurriness—gain the reader's trust.

SC: Thank you for saying that. Honesty is important to me when it comes to memoir writing, or else the story becomes fiction. I should say upfront I am not a big fan of composite characters or changing things that the writer deems necessary to improve the story and small enough that the reader won't mind. I don't believe in making up dialogue or making up scenes. If I didn't remember something or write it down at the time it happened, it did not go into my memoir as "truth." I realize memory is inherently flawed, but I wanted the reader to know that if something went into my book, that was how I recalled it. Readers could at least trust that. We could talk on and on about what is truth versus Truth, and how my memory of events will be different from another person's. But I'm a big believer in—at the very least—being honest with what you do and don't remember. When I couldn't remember something well, I sometimes used, as the great memoirist Rebecca McClanahan taught me to do, "the gift of perhaps," which explicitly signals to the reader that *what I am about to tell you clearly resides in the realm of my imagination,* and therefore I didn't hock it as truth.

I wish I had a perfect memory. I was fortunate to still have my journals from over the years, and those helped a great deal, but there were two stories from my life that I really wanted to include in this memoir that I couldn't recall well enough—in terms of dialogue specifically—to do them justice. Instead, I chose not to include them and then wrote them as fiction instead. They are now part of the short story collection I am working on, and both have been accepted for publication in literary magazines.

AM: What are your hobbies outside of writing?

SC: I love dancing, when I manage to make it to a dance. I read, I walk a ton, and I jog the occasional few miles. I keep a garden, though I'm no expert at it. I absolutely love hiking, and I seem to travel quite a bit.

AM: You hold an M.F.A. Do you feel that aspiring writers should pursue these programs?

SC: I think that MFA programs can be a huge benefit to writers. I'm grateful for my MFA—there's no question it made me a better writer, and I am still very tight with my peers from the program. I don't believe in shoulds, though, and I don't believe an MFA program is necessary to pursue becoming an author. It certainly can help, but the main thing is being dogged about one's writing, not giving up. This writing stuff takes grit, and rejection is all around for the taking. But if you have grit, the rejection becomes less important. You shrug at it and move on.

AM: Do you have personal strategies or tactics for maintaining grit?

SC: In terms of writing, yes: I don't take rejections personally and therefore they don't crush me—98% of the time. The other 2% happens when someone I really respect tears apart a work of mine I love. What can I say? I'm not perfect.

I write for me most if not all of the time—that is, for the fun of it rather than with an endgame in mind. This allows me the freedom to experience the joy that got me started writing in the first place, and it is why, to this day, I continue to love writing.

AM: I've loved reading your writing. Thanks for doing this interview. Please do keep writing, for everyone's sake.

Robert P. Waxler

AM: **I'm grateful for this interview, Bob. As you know, I read and enjoyed your book** *The Risk of Reading*. **Your latest, coauthored with Martha Pennington, is titled** *Why Reading Books Still Matters* **and addresses themes you've undertaken in the past. One would hope that reading books wouldn't need any defense, but apparently that's not the case.**

RW: Thanks, Allen. Yes, part of the problem is the screen culture, the speed and power of it, the way it distracts and disembodies, fragments our attention, distances us from the depth of ourselves. Screens invite us to watch, to surf the current that pulls us along. By contrast, books, especially literature (which is the focus of our interest here), slow us down, offer an opportunity to be attentive, to feel the pulse of human experience, to become self-reflective. That is "the power of literature in Digital Times" (the subtitle of our book).

So when Martha and I talk about "reading books," we are not talking merely about the books silently sitting on the shelf, but something alive, something that calls to the reader, something that invites dialogue and discussion, something that can excite the deepest dimensions of our imagination, and something that, once actively engaged, can stir the human heart.

In the first part of our book, we examine the digital world, its meaning and implications, living life onscreen and online, its impact on education and literacy. Too often, we find the digital world diminished and dehumanized. Then, we counter this kind of life, exploring the value and ongoing importance of reading fiction and poetry, arguing that literature still provides us with the best chance to preserve our human identity, to build a truly democratic society, to know the depth and dignity of ourselves.

AM: It's important to point out that you and Martha don't deny that digital technology offers benefits and relieves burdens. But you are sober about its function, effects, and potential. You focus on its negatives, which are all too often ignored or overlooked. What are some of these?

RW: Yes, Martha and I certainly acknowledge the benefits of digital technology and the screen culture, but we are particularly concerned with the way great books (especially literary fiction and poetry) have been pushed to the margins as the screen culture has gained control over our lives. We argue that the deep reading of significant literature is a countercultural activity, a way of preserving what we think of as the enduring human values, now threatened by the overuse of digital media.

Literature, for example, offers us an opportunity to experience the complexity and multi-dimensionality of our human identity through language and narrative; digital media, by contrast, seems to offer a much more restricted and surface sense of self, with an emphasis on visual images and flickering screens. In a similar context, "great books" offer us a journey to enrichment, a discovery of beauty and truth, as well as a serious encounter with our vulnerability, even mortality; by contrast, digital technology seems to offer endless entertainment, popular culture for consumption, the "pop and bling" of short-term sensation and perpetual now. The screen culture, with its visual images and algorithms, privileges efficiency and speed over thoroughness and dedicated time; it emphasizes quantification and measurement, cleverness and smartness, rather than knowledge and wisdom.

We also need to consider the way we interact with our screens and the way we interact with literary books. Google, Amazon, Facebook (and so on) control our lives much the way a GPS system controls our driving from one place to another. When we use a GPS system, we do not internalize the experience—it's a disembodied experience we might say. We outsource our body and mind to the machine. As a result, if we try to take the same route without the GPS system, we often do not know where we are; we are lost.

By contrast, when we read a book deeply, we feel a personal resonance; we embody the experience as if we are enacting the language. We listen to the voice of the narrator, but we also control, as Birkerts has pointed out, the rhythm of the reading experience, moving at our own bodily rhythm and pace. We participate in the unfolding story, making it part of us. The story, in other words, lives within us, even after we close the book itself. One result of all this is that we learn about ourselves, gain personal knowledge, expand our possibilities.

In addition, I would say that, in general, screen culture is fixated on the present moment and offers little sense of temporal coherence or spatial rootedness. When we rapidly move from one screen to the next, we might experience an impulse or temporary sensation, information for short-term memory, perhaps. Engaged in language unfolding in a novel, though, we experience the past and the present, anticipate the future, and we sense a location in time. We are attentive through time, and so can make the reading experience part of our long-term memory, part of our expanding human identity.

AM: Lately I've read articles about the decline of e-book and Kindle sales and the concomitant increase in traditional book sales. Amazon is now moving to brick-and-mortar stores. I wonder if consumers are aware, at least at some level, of the conditions you've mentioned.

RW: The print book does seem to be surviving in Digital Times, but what that actually means is somewhat difficult to gauge. The e-book offers portability and convenience, for example. You can carry several books at the same time on a small electronic device. By comparison, people seem to prefer print books when they are reading to children or want to share books with others. Students tell me that they also like e-books because they are less expensive than print books, but if they want to stay attentive and really "get into the book," then they prefer print. Print books foster an embodied experience. You can feel the paper, flip the pages back and forth with your fingers, develop a spatial sense of where what you read earlier in the book is located. Even the smell of the book makes a difference. The screen distances the reader from the text—and, I would say, from the voice of the author as well. It fosters a disembodied experience.

It is also interesting to consider how and what people are reading. People are not reading the same kind of books they read in the past. As my co-author Martha likes to remind me, most people are "reading lite" rather than "reading heavy." The reading level of books is lower, they are shorter, the level of editing is down, and self-published books are now common, often furthering the values of consumerism and popular culture rather than literary art.

There is also a tendency to read faster when using e-books, to read on the surface rather than move deeply into the flow of the reading experience, and to multitask while reading, with one hand free to do other things, distracting the reader from the depth of the story unfolding through the language of the book itself. In fact, the e-book seems to reduce the imaginative act of reading—what makes reading difficult but especially rewarding when successful. Unlike the physicality and sensuous quality of print books, the e-book often diminishes the attentive focus necessary to fully absorb the details that transport us into the meaningful pleasure of great books.

Part of the problem is that the screen culture has become the mainstream culture, favoring the visual over the textual, privileging images over words. Reading online, and through screens, affects the way we behave, and so the way we read now. Quick absorption of information rather than slow and thoughtful processing is typical of the current behavior, often celebrated as smartness and efficient thinking. The e-book as a device encourages such behavior, at times despite itself.

In general, e-reading on electronic devices is worthwhile if you are reading for bits of information, but if you are attempting to gain knowledge, seeking wisdom to "know thyself," then print books, especially literary narrative and poetry, continue to have the advantage. As Max Bruinsma once put it, "screens are for watching, paper for reading."

AM: Do you think the quality of writing for magazines and news media has degenerated as well? Would this decline, if it exists, be a symptom of what we're talking about?

RW: "Writing-lite" is the flip side of "reading-lite"—that is, in one sense, writing is reading, and reading is writing—so it follows that if reading is degenerating, then writing is degenerating as well. Furthermore, writing for most magazines and news media has always been writing to provide fleeting information to readers, not necessarily to engage in significant dialogue that might lead to a grasp of long-term knowledge and truth. Most magazines and news media outlets in Digital Times do not make long-form attempts to capture an enduring truth. They offer short articles, easily consumed, ephemeral, almost empty texts. Admittedly, this is not a new problem, but it has been exacerbated by screens and electronic devices. Walter Benjamin was talking about it a century or so ago: "The value of information does not survive the moment in which it is news. It lives only at that moment; it has to surrender to it completely and explain itself to it without losing any time." Writing for most magazines and news media has now become an exercise in the process of forgetting—an offer, quick and easy, a form of distraction, entertainment to be consumed.

Much writing today is governed by the same screen-culture behavior we have been discussing; it is not writing for discovery, but for entertainment, the "pop and bling" lifestyle (as Martha likes to put it), the shiny object that ushers in the emptiness of celebrity, the glitter without human meaning or purpose. There are a few magazines that still honor the long-form in print, but they are the rare exceptions. At times, they offer something well-earned, something original to think about. By contrast, cable news networks seem primarily interested in creating "hives" of readers/listeners, simply offering the same images over and over again to an audience already supporting the ideology of the network. They count on their followers to agree, not necessarily to think.

Writing online obviously is targeting readers online, and both writing and reading are changed by the digital screen. Sound files and video clips, even commercial advertising, often interrupt the flow of the text, for example, making reading and writing fragmented and jumpy. Short words, short sentences, short paragraphs, tweets struggling against visual effects, hyperlinks, bells and whistles—all point to the diminution of language as if the goal is an empty text. Visualized and computerized news and magazines with flash (pop and bling) easily trump the complexity and density of print and long-form articles, in general. As print fades, giving way to digital screens and shortened attention spans, writing loses its complexity, its attempt at discovery and enduring values, its traditional journey into the mysterious depth of human knowledge.

AM: What's the solution, or solutions, to this problem, if any?

RW: Human beings are born with an innate desire to learn, and that learning process includes not only the acquisition of practical skills, information about how to survive and make a living, but also what Socrates claimed as the real goal of learning, the fundamental quest for human knowledge and the good life: to know the self. Socrates was more interested in the "who" than the "what," something deeper and more holistic than what we usually experience with digital gadgets and social media. It should not be surprising that Socrates came up with his ideas without any help from smartphones or the Internet.

Digital technology moves us further and further away from the Socratic sense of what it means to be human and what it is that we really desire to learn. In fact, digital technology seems, too often, to insist that we have no depth, no interior self, no possibility for imaginative and humane coherence, that we are nothing but material goods, what can be measured and quantified. At times, the technology likes to tell us what we desire before we even have a chance to focus our attention on it.

Martha and I believe that encounters with great literature can provide at least a glimpse of what Socrates and other traditional thinkers advocate. Digital technology is clearly an important part of the world today, but literature, and the humanities in general, offers a counterweight to the rampant speed and power that digital devices insist on. Our schools, for example, should create a balanced curriculum, giving much more emphasis than they usually do to fiction and poetry, to books without the use of digital devices, to the kind of activity that acknowledges that something in ourselves, deep down, connects to other human beings, makes us human.

Literature is not a magic bullet, a single solution to the complex issues of our Digital Times, but literature is essential to human life and education. Without it, we are diminished, hollowed out, increasingly becoming nodes on an electronic grid. Books make us human.

Books, and the culture of books that gives a place to literature and language (rather than screens and images), should be recognized as a central part of our critical heritage and a superior resource for learning. The visual experience is very powerful in human beings, but we seem now to be drawn obsessively to the visual, to the flashing, colorful computer screen, the pop and bling lifestyle. We need to be more attentive to language, especially literary language. Unlike the language of the media, of politics, of advertising, which seeks to control and manipulate others, literary language encourages empathy and compassion, various perspectives, multi-dimensional possibilities, and a variety of individual interpretations.

Martha and I are convinced that in today's world, people need space and time in schools and in public places where they shut off their electronic gadgets, where they quietly read works of great literature, and where they discuss that literature in the presence of other human beings, face-to-face. Like No-Fly Zones, there should be No Wi-Fi Zones, countercultural spaces where literature and language help to maintain the traditional sense of what it means to live a good life and to preserve our humanity.

AM: How would you define great literature? Can technology be used as a force in its service, or are we moving inexorably toward some post-literary future?

RW: Martha and I believe that human story shaped through language significantly contributes to our individual identities and, at the same time, creates connections to the community that we interact with. Story evokes story, builds community, and we locate ourselves through the stories that we hear and tell. Language and story, when working well, are like a covenant between us and others, heart-felt and deep, helping to give us purpose and direction. Great literature has much of the same quality.

The kind of literature we are talking about is not just for entertainment, but for discovery, not for consumption but for questing and questioning. It has an aesthetic authority and personal resonance, appealing in its vibrant language and rhythm. You can read the same work a hundred times, and each time you will be surprised by it, find something new in it, be startled by it, wonder how you missed the meaning of this detail or that one.

Unlike commercial and most genre fiction, great literature cannot be consumed, and it will not consume you. Yet great literature can be considered dangerous, at times risky, taking the reader on a quest into unknown territory, offering a glimpse of the unfamiliar. Through the quality of the language—metaphor, metonymy, synecdoche, irony—this kind of literature has the capacity to make the familiar strange, and the strange familiar, to evoke memory, to read us as we read it. Unlike popular and commercial literature, great literature demands our time and attention. It draws us to what cannot be measured or defined—not commercialized or quantified. It is implicit rather than explicit, not asserting solutions to problems, but offering significant questions that need to be pondered. That is part of its pleasure and joy.

An encounter with the richly textured aesthetic language of books is as challenging as it is fulfilling. It helps keep us human, in part at least because, at its best, it moves us beyond cultural and political differences, makes us more empathetic and more willing to acknowledge our shared vulnerability and mortality.

It does seem as if we are moving toward some kind of post-literary future. But Martha and I do not think this is inevitable. Each generation produces great readers, curious minds that desire to join the adventure of reading great books. There will always be people who believe in books, as long as books are there for them to be called. Mobile devices and other electronic gadgets could serve books, too, I suppose—mainly by pointing out why reading books still matters.

Johnnie Bernhard

AM: You've been a regular contributor to *Southern Literary Review*, Johnnie, so I'm particularly happy for the occasion to interview you about your new novel, *A Good Girl*. Tell us about Gracey Reiter.

JB: Gracey Reiter is the protagonist for my work of historical fiction, *A Good Girl*. A middle-aged woman, Gracey is conflicted by crossroads in her career, marriage, and family relationships. Her conflicts are universal to the human condition – the loss of innocence in youth, the emotional difficulty of aging parents, and life's meaning as one ages. Woven into this conflict is the story of six generations of an Irish-German immigrant family. The reader will discover these same universal conflicts with each generation, compounded by significant events such as wars, the Great Depression, hurricanes, and other political and economic events.

Gracey reflects upon the lives of her mother, grandmother, and great grandmothers and finds strength and wisdom. The male characters of the novel are complex characters, as well. Gracey interacts with them in the role of wife, mother, daughter, and granddaughter. *A Good Girl* is the story of family, two countries, and three centuries. It is the story of self-discovery, as well as of the immigrants' place in American history.

The novel was shortlisted in the Wisdom-Faulkner International Writing Competition, a finalist in the national Kindle Book Award, and a nominee for the 2018 PEN-Bingham Prize. It was chosen for panel discussion at the 2017 Mississippi and Louisiana Book Festivals.

AM: Was it difficult to alternate time periods? Did you have a strategy for keeping the narratives straight?

JB: My strategy for alternating between time periods was based on a common thread woven through all six generations. It is the Bible of Aileen Walsh of Galway, Ireland, the matriarch of the Walsh-Mueller family. The family Bible is passed down to the next generation, ensuring all six generations have taken part in not only viewing the family tree printed on the opening page of the Bible, but also adding to it. The family tree begins with Aileen Walsh of Galway, Ireland in 1830 and ends with Patricia Grace of Forkhill, Ireland in 2015. This family's immigration story makes a complete circle.

The second connecting thread was a hand embroidered handkerchief with the initials AW owned by the matriarch of the family. This handkerchief is passed down to all the women in the family. It evidently becomes a wedding gift for the American daughter returning to Ireland in 2015.

Perhaps the main organizational tool I used was a complete character sketch of each character that included physical attributes, emotional attributes, the era in which they lived, including social and economic issues, and the clothes that he or she may have worn.

My historical research was based on information from the Texas State Historical Association and online articles in the *Galway Advertiser* of Galway, Ireland.

AM: Have you traveled through Ireland?

JB: I have been to Ireland many times. I adore the people and the culture. Their sense of pride, resilience, and hospitality is second to none.

AM: You used to teach. Did you teach writing?

JB: I taught high school English, including AP English, but I began my writing career as a journalist in Houston many years ago. I believe the dual degrees taught me valuable skills in writing, including the use of sensory details and the economy of words in narration. I most recently taught a writing course at the University of Southern Mississippi. As an author, I attend many conferences teaching workshops and participating in panel discussions on writing and literature. I enjoy working with writers.

AM: Does *A Good Girl* attempt to teach anything?

JB: The teaching components would be in the novel's multiple themes of the immigrant story in America, the importance of family, and the power of self-discovery.

AM: This is your debut novel. How did you write it? I mean right down to the basics—did you use a computer? A pen? A typewriter? Did you have a writing routine?

JB: *A Good Girl* is my debut novel. My second novel, *How We Came to Be*, is set for release in May 2018. I am traditionally published by Texas Review Press, a university press in partnership with Texas A&M University Press.

My best energy is in the early morning. This is when I write. I am fortunate to have an office with a lot of natural light. I compose on the computer, but also have note pads in my purse, as well as other places in the house. I never know when I'll get an idea.

The interesting thing about writing is when you hit the sweet spot, the manuscript takes on a life of its own. There were times I'd wake up in the middle of the night and write. Some days I'd accomplish a paragraph or two, while others I wrote a chapter. The editing process with multiple drafts is just as important as the writing. I had a beta reader and participated in a critique group during the editing process. This is before working with the editor at the publishing house.

AM: For those who don't know, what's a beta reader?

JB: A beta reader is an unpaid reader who reads your manuscript, offering suggestions on dialogue, plot, theme, characterization, etc. In return for this service, you read the manuscript of the beta reader. This is not developmental or copy editing, but rather an overall review of the manuscript. It is important to align genres and skills with your beta reader, ensuring a fair exchange of work.

AM: This is probably as good a time as any to mention that you not only write but also help other writers.

JB: I do enjoy helping other writers. I understand the arduous task of writing, editing, publishing, and marketing. It is a very difficult business to break into, as well as sustain. Of course, the more you know about the business, the better off you are.

Attend conferences, participate in critique groups, and read the masters of your genre. The most important advice I can give to any writer is to believe in the story you are writing. This passion will sustain you despite the rejections from literary agents and publishers. It's all part of it.

AM: Have you had any mentors who were writers?

JB: My favorite authors are Barbara Kingsolver, Walker Percy, and William Faulkner. Of course, there are many authors I currently read, beyond the mastery of those three. I learn something from each one. It could be an interesting sentence pattern or the use of sensory detail.

AM: You seem to have a knack for dialogue.

JB: Writing dialogue is about listening carefully to what others say. People do not use complete sentences when they speak. I often read dialogue out loud during the editing process, so I can best judge how "natural" it is.

AM: Well, I appreciate the time you took to dialogue with me. Thanks, Johnnie.

Steve Wiegenstein

AM: So glad *Southern Literary Review* has a chance to feature your work again, Steve. Thanks for doing this interview. I bet when you wrote this book, you couldn't have anticipated how timely a story about a post-Civil War 19th century community would be. If you turn on the news these days, you see ongoing debates and demonstrations involving the history of the period the book covers.

SW: Allen, it's great to talk to you, and I appreciate the opportunity to talk about my work.

Surely the events of the last couple of months have disabused us all of the notion that historical fiction isn't "relevant." Historians have rightly taken the lead in helping us understand the significance of the artifacts and memorials that surround us and which, I suspect, many people never gave much thought to, but I think the novelists have a part to play in pursuing that understanding as well.

The historian can tell us how and why a particular event occurred, but the novelist probably has a better shot at expressing what it felt like to be there. Both perspectives are important. It seems to me that we are lately being reminded that the ownership of the past—including ownership of the stories of the past—is an important element in the control of the present.

AM: Reminds me of the Faulkner line: "The past is never dead. It's not even past." What drew you to this particular period? I should note for readers that this book is the third installment in a series.

SW: My novels are set in the Ozarks, and the years 1887-

88, when *The Language of Trees* takes place, are significant in Ozarks history. That's when large economic interests from the East came and established logging and mining operations in the region on a scale much greater than ever before. This industrial approach to extraction (especially timber harvesting) altered the culture, devastated the landscape, and changed the way in which people could make a living. It was a kind of rapid-pace microcosm of the coming of the modern era in society, so for me it was a great time period to focus on.

So many themes just lying there waiting to be picked up, and a historical period that isn't overdone. The clearing of the Ozarks timber in the late 19th and early 20th centuries was one of those quiet, little-noticed environmental catastrophes that should be better known, so it made a good backdrop for the doings of my characters.

AM: Let's talk about those characters—the Turners and Josephine Mercadier and all the rest. Philip Roth once told an interviewer, "Beginning a book is unpleasant. I'm entirely uncertain about the character and the predicament, and a character in his predicament is what I have to begin with." Can you relate?

SW: I can't say that I do. To me, the uncertainty one feels when working through a book is intensely thrilling. It's the closest I'll ever get to walking the high wire. And the comparison is apt: with major characters, I usually have a goal in mind—this one is headed for a moral failure; that one needs to fall insanely in love; this one is going to turn out to be much stronger than anyone ever expected—but how I'm going to get to that goal is not always clear. And focusing too much on the particular mechanics of a character's development is the writerly equivalent of looking down at your feet. You have to keep your eyes focused on the distant target and trust intuition to guide your steps. It's not like tightrope walking in that I'm not risking death or serious injury, and if I misstep I can always rip out a few chapters and try again, but it is an enormously exciting sensation to venture out into the unknown with a set of characters.

AM: *The Language of Trees* is your third book. I mentioned earlier that it's the third installment in a series. I've

heard it said that the first book you write is always the toughest to finish. Has that been your experience? Have you found it easier to write these last two installments?

SW: Honestly, it's getting harder. The task gets more complicated with each book. With *Slant of Light*, I had a clean slate to create characters and a storyline, and *This Old World* was written in essentially a continuous run with it. But *The Language of Trees* jumps the story ahead twenty years, so although many characters persist from the first two books, I have to think anew about them while keeping them consistent with what's been established already. The book has to be rewarding for both first-time readers and repeat readers, with the widely differing demands of each type. And finally, I'm hoping that themes introduced in the earlier books will begin to show themselves in full, but that's the sort of thing you don't want people to notice in an obvious way, so I found myself doing much more of a juggling act with plot, setting, and story than I had before.

The next book, which I am working on now, jumps ahead another fifteen years or so, but at this point it's not proving to be quite as daunting. Maybe I'm getting used to the added layers of complexity that come from multiple books in a connected series, or maybe I just haven't hit the hard part yet.

AM: Who's your favorite novelist?

SW: Can I say "for certain purposes"? Because I love a lot of novelists for different things. For his incredible word sense and ability to build entire worlds, and to encapsulate human history into an intensely local and specifically defined region, I have to say Faulkner. But for innovative structure and an absolutely hypnotic ability to draw me in and make me live in the novel for weeks at a time, I'd go with W. G. Sebald.

From my own part of the country, Donald Harington is my favorite. He's a remarkably audacious writer who has something new to say with each book, and I love his style even though we're nothing alike stylistically. I admire his willingness to discount the demands of plot, and that's not to say that his books don't have plots. But so many writers seem compelled to advance the plot on every page, which has always seemed to me to be a very constricted approach; I suspect that's the influence of movies and TV, which are very plot-driven media, at work on the minds of writers.

Overall, though, for intellectual heftiness, outrageously perfect verbal choices, and unforgettable stories, I think Herman Melville is my favorite. You can see him straining at the bonds of possibility with every book.

AM: Do you find yourself reading to become a better writer, or do you just read for leisure and hope for sublimation of skill in the process?

SW: I'd have to say that I've never read with a conscious idea for picking up techniques or ideas, although like all writers, I'm sure there's a lot of unconscious osmosis. Now that I think about it, none of the novelists I mentioned earlier has a style anything like mine, so I guess I read them for the difference, not their similarity.

I think my style was formed by my early days as a newspaper reporter, when economy and precision were the highest values, and the goal was to say as much as possible in the fewest possible words. I've always admired the style of John Williams, the author of *Butcher's Crossing, Augustus,* and *Stoner.* He's a classical stylist who rarely uses figures of speech, but when he brings one into a sentence, it always packs a wallop.

In terms of theme and subject, I draw more from nonfiction than from other fiction writers; Thoreau and Emerson have always been my touchstones in terms of the American heart, and I draw on a lot of contemporary history writers. I'd particularly call attention to David Thelen's *Paths of Resistance,* which is about the ways in which ordinary people resisted the relentless pressure of corporatization and homogenization in the late nineteenth and early twentieth centuries, and Aaron Astor's *Rebels on the Border,* which deals with the reintegration of the border states after the Civil War.

AM: May we expect more books from you? Are you working on anything in particular at the moment?

SW: I'm working on a novel that will bring the series into the twentieth century, specifically the years 1903-1904. That historical moment is meaningful to me because those are the years of the Louisiana Purchase Exposition, better known as the St. Louis World's Fair, when American triumphalism was celebrated in a grand and ostentatious way.

The "American Century" was beginning then, and there was such faith in technological progress and the superiority of the U.S. way of life. Frighteningly dark undercurrents were also present in the fair, most notably in the exhibition of "primitive societies" that, frankly, celebrated white supremacy. The U.S. had recently acquired the Philippines in the Spanish-American War, and at the fair the Philippine exhibit was by far the largest. Other cultures, such as the Pygmy and Ainu, were put on display as well, so that white Americans could gawk and celebrate their "innate superiority."

In *The Language of Trees*, there's a sense that technology has replaced social culture as the chief driver of utopian sentiment, so this book will pick up that thread. The inhabitants of Daybreak, living just a short train ride from St. Louis, will be involved in the fair, and I'm looking forward to developing some of the themes of urban versus rural and agrarian versus industrial that have cropped up in *The Language of Trees*.

AM: I look forward to reading the next installment. Thanks for the interview. Happy writing.

Dan Leach

AM: Congratulations on the publication of your collection of stories, *Floods and Fires*. We share a publisher—the University of North Georgia Press—as well as a connection to Greenville, South Carolina, where I went to school at Furman. You graduated from Clemson in 2008. Were you writing stories then?

DL: Thanks, Allen. Congratulations to you, as well. I look forward to reading *The Southern Philosopher*.

With respect to your question, "stories" would be too generous a term for what I was writing back in 2008. In love with literature and intent on joining the conversation, I was definitely attempting to write them. I'd play with phrasing or produce little vignettes or sketches. I'd sometimes tinker with poetry. But I hadn't hung around long enough. I hadn't read enough good books.

It wasn't until 2012 that I wrote "The Day Getting Dark," which was the first thing I'd done that I was proud of, that I'd set beside Barry Hannah or Ron Rash and not feel bad about.

AM: Sam Baker wrote a piece in *The Telegraph* about three years ago in which he claimed that the short story, as a genre, is "having a moment." Do you think that's true?

DL: As someone who writes little else, I certainly hope that Sam's right. I've heard it observed that the best screenwriters are leaving film and making a mass exodus into television. I think you could make the same argument for fiction, couldn't you? Many of the writers I'd consider the best of our time—George Saunders, Junot Diaz, and Richard Ford, to name a few—

are devoting as much or more energy to their short stories as they are their novels. Combine that with our culture's ever-dwindling attention span and I think it's possible that a long overdue "moment" has arrived for the short story. And then there's Alice Munro, a pure short story writer, winning the Nobel Prize. So—who knows?—maybe Sam's got it.

AM: Funny you mention screenwriters. I noticed that Tom Hanks—yes, *that* Tom Hanks—has just written a collection of short stories.

DL: Tom Hanks making the move into short fiction? Without having read his stuff, I'm imagining something slightly better than James Franco but nowhere near as good as Miranda July. That's interesting, though.

Anyone who works in film must have at least decent instincts for story, dialogue, and pacing, right? What will be interesting to see is the quality of the prose, especially on the sentence level. Because that kind of command, as you know, comes only after so many countless hours wrestling with the language. Who knows, though? Maybe all these years Tom's been honing his craft. What is your expectation? More or less optimistic than if Cormac McCarthy suddenly announced he was starring in a film?

AM: I don't have an expectation, really, but I suspect Hanks had some help with the writing. One thing I like about *your* collection—to get back to the subject—is its varying narrative styles. For example, the opening story is told in the third person while the confessional first-person narrator in the second story probably seems more sophisticated to the reader than he does to the characters that populate his fictional world.

DL: Good eye. Shortly after the collection was accepted by UPNG, I reached out to several mentors regarding how to order the stories. I got some fine advice from George Singleton and Dale Ray Phillips, both of whom have been very generous with me. But it was Bret Lott who recommended avoiding the temptation to "frontload," that is putting your strongest work first and following it in descending order of quality. Instead Bret advised ordering the stories based on narrators. He said to be aware of the balance between 1st and 3rd person voice, but also of the narrators' ages and voices. I listened, so it pleases me a great deal when a sharp reader such as yourself picks up on it.

AM: Singleton and Phillips and Lott—you've had some excellent mentors, each with a Carolina connection.

DL: There's a great story about how all that came about. I mentioned earlier that it wasn't until 2012 that I wrote my first "true" story. Well, I wrote it shortly after my first daughter had been born. Though healthy, she was a fussy kid and had her days and nights flipped around. Luckily, she was born in summer, which meant that I was on break from teaching.

Anyway, she was asleep on my chest, I was reading Singleton's *The Half-Mammals of Dixie,* and, out of the ether, an idea for a story popped into my head. I opened up a Word document and started typing. Two hours later, I had finished "The Day Getting Dark." I read it over and, with the exception of a few hiccups in the plot, I was relatively pleased. I wanted to do something with it, but, having virtually no knowledge of the publishing process (and being too proud to type something like that into a search engine), I did what, at the time, seemed natural. I looked up George Singleton's email address (actually tracked it down on the staff directory on Wofford College's web page) and sent the story to him. This all happened sometime between 3 and 4 in the morning.

I had no idea how audacious this was and have since blamed sleep-deprivation.

To make a long story short, George answered. He read the story and liked it enough to send it to his friend Denton Loving, who at the time ran d*rafthorse* literary magazine. Publishing gave me a much needed sense of validation, and I wrote a few more stories. George read them all and gave me some incredible feedback. Then, he put me in touch with Dale Ray Phillips. Not only did Dale Ray run one of my stories in *The Madrid Review,* but he has been reading my stuff ever since and basically giving me an MFA through emails.

To me, those guys are the best in the world at what they do. It'd be like being mentored by Hemingway in the 1920's or Cheever in the 1960's.

AM: I confess to feeling jealous.

DL: Keith Morris over at Clemson recently set me up with a young and talented writer named Stephen Hundley. I've been mentoring him for several months and recently celebrated with him over his first publication—a dark and hilarious Civil War piece called "Replica" that ran in *Driftwood*. Though no Singleton or Lott, I'm trying my best to pay forward some of the kindness and support that has been so generously shown to me. Hundley, by the way, is going to be huge. You read it here first.

AM: Where are you these days? Are you writing full-time or are you like the rest of us mortals who have regular jobs?

DL: As far as the writing life goes, I'm as mortal as it gets. As we speak, I'm on the clock at a large insurance company where I work as a claims adjuster. As you might imagine, this interview has been the highlight of my day. What did Dickey say of his advertising job? Something like "I sold my soul to the Devil every day and wrote like hell every night to buy it back." That's me.

In all seriousness, I think my writing life has been better than ever since leaving teaching. I graduated from Clemson with an education degree in 2008 and worked in the classroom until October 2016. Summers and breaks were great for getting work done, but otherwise teaching sapped me pretty badly. I remember reading an Updike interview in which he said, "Whatever brain cells are required to write are the first ones killed when you step in a classroom." Strong words from a man who taught, if I'm not mistaken, a single summer course at Harvard.

I mentioned Stephen Hundley earlier, the young man I've been mentoring. He recently asked me how and when the work gets done. I confessed to him and I'll confess now to you: "I don't know." I'm not a particularly regimented person, so it happens in short bursts and whatever windows open up between work and kids and wife and the general wildness of life. It honestly baffles me when, after several months, I realize that I've completed several stories. I just keep showing up and, somehow, the work gets done.

AM: I strongly dislike this question, but I'm asking it anyway because I want to know the answer: Do you have a favorite story in this collection?

DL: Actually, I do. "Not Home Yet." And I say that because of its "moments." Maybe more than anything else, when I tell a story, that's what I'm after. There's probably a better, more literary word for what I'm referring to, but I don't know it. By "moments," I mean those points in a story where some combination of crisp imagery and narrative action (possibly even of symbolic motion) bring the reader to the sense that something powerful is underway and that they themselves are being moved by it.

To use several inestimable examples: Nick seeing Gatsby reaching for the green light; Harry Angstrom bolting through the woods at the end of *Rabbit, Run;* or the table scene from "What We Talk About When We Talk About Love." That's my general measure for how good something is: what moments it leaves you with. In "Not Home Yet," there are some I'm really proud of—for instance, in the opening scene where the couple comes home and discovers the dead hen lying in the gravel; the neighbor's various intrusions from his dark porch; and that climax when the protagonist has the shotgun against Bruce's head. Those are what I enjoy writing because those are what I enjoy reading.

A close second? "My Time at the Bottom." It's too "voicey" and will probably not engage readers like some of the more plot-driven pieces like "Transportation" or "Floods and Fires." However, there's some phrasing in that one I absolutely love.

AM: You've got much to be proud of, and I highly recommend these stories to our readers.

DJ Donaldson

AM: Thanks for doing this interview, Don, and congratulations on the publication of your latest in the Andy Broussard mystery series, *Assassination at Bayou Sauvage*. How has this series developed over the years?

DD: The first book, *Cajun Nights*, was a very strange story, partially because the editor at St. Martins, who ultimately bought it, asked me to write a "creepier" ending than what I initially provided. The result was a blend of stark science brought hard up against elements of the paranormal. This combination, which was apparently viewed as fresh and different, caused a reviewer in Booklist to say, "We close this remarkable, intoxicating book like a first-time visitor leaves New Orleans: giddy, a bit disoriented and much less confident in our own assumptions about life."

Now that's a pretty good review. But, being from a science background, I felt self-conscious about relying so much on paranormal possibilities to fuel the story. So, in the next book, while there was still a bit of a paranormal feel to the tale, the resolution of the mystery was entirely anchored in reality.

In the third book and all those thereafter, the stories are firmly based on real forensic science with only a *hint* of the paranormal appearing in the form of Grandma Oustellette, the big Cajun woman who owns the restaurant where my main character, Chief Medical Examiner, Andy Broussard, eats at least one meal a day. Grandma O has "premonitions" that always come true. If she tells Broussard something is about to happen, he listens, even though he doesn't understand how this works.

AM: What is your science background?

DD: I have a PhD in anatomy from the Tulane Medical School in New Orleans. After graduate school, I became an anatomy instructor and eventually, full professor of anatomy at the University of Tennessee Health Science Center in Memphis. For over 40 years there, I taught Microscopic Anatomy to freshman medical and dental students, and conducted an active research program in wound healing.

AM: There's a lot of talk about competition between science and the humanities these days. And yet you've managed to bridge the divide.

DD: Maybe all that means is that the "divide" is more apparent than real. Or you're giving me more credit than I deserve. I'm simply telling stories that arise out of my science background. I haven't left my formal training and experience behind by becoming a novelist. I'm just making use of it in a somewhat non-traditional way. But thanks for the compliment.

AM: Let's turn back to the novel. The catalyst for the twists and turns of plot is the murder of Andy's uncle, Joe. I want to avoid spoilers in this interview, so let me put the question this way: how do you craft the narrative surprises? Do you map out Andy's story beforehand, or do you just write and hope the storyline develops as you go?

DD: In each of my books there's a central idea I want to write about. Usually, it's some interesting medical issue that I've spent a lot of time researching. The one at the heart of this story required me to construct an extensive family tree for my main character, Andy Broussard, including the sex, name, and age of about 50 people. This work falls into the category of preproduction. I believe it's also important in each story to make sure my two main characters change in some way as a result of what happens to them. I typically have a good idea of what these little character arcs will entail before I start writing.

From this point, I'd compare my process to a family taking a car trip from Steubenville, Ohio, to the Grand Canyon. These folks obviously know all about their starting point and have a fairly good idea what their destination will look like. Along the way they plan to stop at the biggest Lego-brick dinosaur on earth. Additionally, they want to see the planet's largest sweater collection woven from belly-button lint. Beyond that, they'll keep their eyes open along the way for signs advertising other attractions of interest. Might even be willing to go a few miles out of the way for a really compelling sight.

Sitting at the keyboard, ready to begin this book, I could see the opening scene clearly and knew exactly what was going on behind the scene. That knowledge carried me through the first six chapters. Like the family from Steubenville, I knew a couple of other stops I wanted to make on my way to the big finale, but unlike that family, I didn't know how to get there.

Once I have a story rolling, it's mostly a matter of figuring out the next logical step, always keeping in mind that I need some misdirection as I go, a few surprises, a little humor, and whatever character arcs I've decided on. If you're thinking to yourself that this approach relies on a good bit of luck to succeed, I'd agree. But somehow, it always works out.

AM: You could also say that about Andy's sleuthing, right? A little bit of luck here and there, and it always works out.

DD: I'm sorry, but I can't accept the suggestion that a scattering of lucky events explains how Broussard is able to have such a great influence on the resolution of his cases. That notion is contrary to everything he stands for. Broussard is an emotionally flawed intellectual that through his great knowledge and perceptive abilities can see things at murder scenes others can't. He's also able to assemble apparently disparate facts into a meaningful pattern that ultimately leads to the culprit. Luck? I think not.

AM: Okay, so luck isn't a part of it. But what do you think makes Andy so knowledgeable and perceptive? Is that just the way he is, or did he learn and earn his skills?

DD: His high IQ is genetic. His parents were reasonably intelligent people, but gave no outward indication they could produce something like him. That's the beauty of genetics: the recombination of hidden traits can sometimes produce wondrous surprises. That's not to say his abilities can be traced to a single golden gene. They reflect a myriad of combinations that, though highly unlikely to occur in one individual, give him various skills that together make him an extremely rare bird. And as you suggest in the latter part of your question, some of these skills made him a more intense student than most. But as I've mentioned earlier, that DNA shuffle left him holding a very poor hand when it comes to outward expressions of affection.

AM: You sometimes talk about Andy as if he's a real person.

DD: I like to think that even now as I'm typing this, he and the rest of the gang are going about their lives in New Orleans and that I merely report on their adventures from time to time as I learn what they've been doing. It helps me make them real to my readers. Maybe I need a CT scan.

AM: Do you and Andy get along? Do you ever find him pulling one way while you want him to go another?

DD: I never have any problems with him. But I sometimes don't agree with Andy's death-investigator sidekick, Kit Franklyn, and her alligator farmer boyfriend, Teddy LaBiche, as they try to advance their relationship. The best course would be for Teddy to continue living a few hours from New Orleans in the little town near his alligator farm. I keep telling Kit that if he moves to New Orleans and they start living together, he's just going to be underfoot and interfere with her work. If he stays where he is, he can still be available whenever she needs him. But you know Kit... headstrong, impulsive...I don't know what else to say to her.

AM: After this interview I have no doubt we'll be seeing more of Andy in the future.

DD: Grandma Oustellette, the big Cajun woman who runs Andy's favorite restaurant, once told him, "Life don't always care about when *you* wanna do things." Keeping that in mind, I will say that after so many years with Andy, it would be hard to say goodbye.

AM: Well, it's hard for me to say goodbye to you after this interview, but I'm afraid I must. Please give Andy my regards.

Kelly Kennington

AM: Thanks for doing this interview. For your book, *In the Shadow of Dred Scott*, which was just published by the University of Georgia Press, you did an extraordinary amount of archival research, including digging through the case files of hundreds of enslaved people, sifting through letters and correspondence, and piecing together execution books and manumission records. On top of that, you reviewed more than 800 state supreme-court freedom suits to place your research into a wider context. This process must have shown that Dred Scott's situation was, sadly, not unique.

KK: Thank you for inviting me to share my book with your readers. Yes, my research indicates that hundreds of enslaved men, women and children from all over the United States sued for freedom in the antebellum era. For example, I located almost 20 published opinions of freedom suits in the Supreme Court of Alabama. In the St. Louis Circuit Court, where I completed the bulk of my archival research, nearly 40 percent of the cases resulted in freedom, including the Scott family.

What is unique about their case is that, in their appeal to the United States Supreme Court, Chief Justice Roger Taney not only failed to find for the Scotts' freedom—despite their use of an argument that had previously been successful in Missouri's courts—he also used the case to deny American citizenship to all African Americans. The Scotts' case has become the most famous of the many freedom suits of this period, but they were not unique or unusual until the opinion in their appeal.

AM: What conclusions did you draw as you moved from looking at individual freedom suits in isolation to viewing them as part of a larger pattern or scheme?

KK: My research has always prioritized the experiences of individuals, so my findings center on the importance of law and legal culture to enslaved people in the city of St. Louis. There and elsewhere, enslaved men and women managed to learn about law, access attorneys and bring cases that resulted in freedom at high rates (38 percent in St. Louis). Freedom suits were also significant because of the many additional battles they initiated—both in and out of the courtroom—including related legal disputes, heated conversations and nervous correspondence from slaveholders desperate to maintain their control. As such, African Americans were active contributors to the legal culture of slavery in antebellum America.

I find that enslaved people had a remarkable ability to transmit information and seek out opportunities to sue in the most advantageous location. The St. Louis example was not unusual, as appellate cases from elsewhere make clear. In addition to finding the existence of a broader legal culture among enslaved individuals than many scholars have recognized, I also argue that judges and juries used these cases to engage in conversations about slavery in their local communities. For this reason, the outcomes of the suits often depended on local conditions and relationships, making it difficult to draw broader conclusions about this type of case outside of the local circumstances of each particular court.

AM: What were some of the legal arguments made by those seeking freedom from enslavement? Were they chiefly constitutional in focus, or were there other bases, say, in contract or property? I would guess many involved manumission laws.

KK: The vast majority of the enslaved plaintiffs in St. Louis argued for freedom based on residence in a free territory or free state, which usually meant Illinois, under the doctrine of "once free, always free" as established in the English case of *Somerset v. Stewart* in 1772. Interstate comity was vital to the successful use of this argument.

An additional set of arguments included disputes over manumissions, such as when a person arranged to buy freedom after a number of years and the slaveholder refused to honor the agreement, or if a slaveholder promised freedom in his or her will, but was in too much debt or the heirs or executors challenged the manumission.

Another group of plaintiffs argued they had always been free, but had been kidnapped and sold into slavery; the most famous of these cases was Solomon Northop, who wrote a memoir that was recently made into the feature film, *Twelve Years a Slave*.

One final argument to mention is the claim that the plaintiff was of Indian ancestry on his or her mother's side, since personal status followed the mother (under the doctrine of *partus sequitur ventrem*) and Missouri and several other states outlawed Indian slavery in the 18th century. There are other grounds used in cases outside of St. Louis, but most of these are based in specific regional legislation, such as laws against moving an enslaved person out of a state for the purpose of sale.

AM: Is it possible to estimate how many of these arguments succeeded and how many failed, or is the research still too fresh in this area?

KK: Yes, we have the numbers for the St. Louis cases, but for the appellate cases, there are too many unknown outcomes for reliable estimates. For purposes of calculating the rates of success in the St. Louis cases, I divided the arguments into three categories: arguments based on residence in a free territory/state; arguments for prior manumission; and arguments for freedom from birth, which includes kidnapping victims and those who claimed Indian ancestry. I compiled the precise numbers in several tables available in the book's appendix. The most successful cases were those based on freedom from birth, where plaintiffs won 49 percent of cases. Residence in free territory resulted in freedom 38 percent of the time, and prior manumission, which included agreements for manumission, resulted in freedom 24 percent of the time.

AM: How did you first become interested in this topic?

KK: I have always been interested in law and history, so I planned to major in history and go to law school after college. While getting my undergraduate degree at Tulane, I took a couple of classes that changed my plans. First, I took visiting Professor Betty Wood's class on "Slavery and Freedom in the Old South," which began my fascination with the ideas of slavery and freedom in the United States, partly because my high school history teachers had not taught me anything about this important topic, but also because I struggled to understand the existence of slavery in a country whose rhetoric had always centered on ideas of liberty. The other class I took was an American legal history class with Dr. Judith Schafer, whose research focused on slavery and the law. Dr. Schafer's course allowed me to see that I could combine my love of law with my love of history.

Dr. Schafer then introduced me to freedom suit research and directed my undergraduate senior thesis on a Louisiana Supreme Court freedom suit, *Eulalie and her children v. Long & Mabry* (1854). In graduate school at Duke, I planned to study slavery in the era of the American Revolution, but then I learned of a federal grant to study freedom suits in St. Louis (because of the importance of *Dred Scott*). I decided to write a master's thesis and then a dissertation studying these cases. The topic allowed me to combine all of my interests—in slavery versus freedom, legal history and the antebellum era—in one book.

AM: Do you think it's important for practicing lawyers today to have an understanding of this period and in particular of the laws of slavery that shaped Southern culture for much of our nation's history?

KK: Absolutely. I think it is important for all Americans to understand slavery because it built much of the wealth and infrastructure of this country, not only in the South, but in all of the U.S.

For attorneys, in particular, understanding the history of African Americans' relationship with the law and with legal authority is key for thinking through how that relationship functions today. I would also expect that a study of legal culture in other times and places is useful for thinking about how the broader population views the legal system today.

I'm sure that modern attorneys will recognize many of the legal forms, arguments and negotiations that make up much of my book. Seeing how these things changed, and how some things have stayed the same, might help lawyers think about the processes of legal development.

Lorna Hollifield

AM: Thanks, Lorna, for doing this interview. The title of your debut novel is *Tobacco Sun*. I want to ask you about that title, but first I want to quote from some opening lines of the book. "Tobacco," you say, "a strangely fragile, yet willful crop, desperate for survivorship, proved it could somehow adapt to the more arid ground in the state's wide middle. No matter the wars fought over top of its sprouts, or the roads built by its stomping grounds, some of the germ always managed to make it another season."

The passage goes on in this lyrical and pensive vein. There's something metaphorical about tobacco here, isn't there?

LH: I consider this my first character introduction. Especially in the South, we seem to be so connected to the places we ran around barefoot as a child. The trees matter, the dirt matters, the agriculture matters, and the people are reflections of it all. In the prologue, by acquainting the audience to the land, I am giving them glimpses into what kind of humans they are about to encounter. The tobacco remains a huge presence and metaphor throughout the novel.

AM: And where did you run around barefoot as a child?

LH: Everywhere! I still hate shoes. I grew up outside of Asheville, North Carolina, in a tiny town called Candler. Summers were spent playing in water hoses and eating watermelon in my grandmother's front yard. I'd also climb our chestnut tree barefoot. That sometimes ended with me crying while mother got the tweezers!

AM: Now you're based in Charleston, right? I once heard Charleston described as a "literary city." Do you think that's the case?

LH: I would say so! I've met many authors from aspiring to best-selling. The city is the current stomping grounds for beach writers like Mary Alice Monroe and Dorothea Benton Frank—and has been the past stomping ground of the great Edgar Allen Poe. The list could go on and on. I think the history coupled with the beautiful scenery kind of makes it the perfect little Petrie dish to grow writers. Literature is part of Charleston's rich culture. I'm proud to be a part of that world.

AM: *Tobacco Sun* tells the story of two sisters from North Carolina after the close of the Second World War. What drew you to this period?

LH: I needed a time period without modern distractions where I could really showcase these salt-of-the-earth personalities. I also like the post-war era because everyone was looking for redemption of some kind. It was a time when the beginnings of modern psychiatry started being explored, which is important for the plot.

AM: Interesting. Do you feel that people are no longer looking for redemption today, or at least not looking for it with the same sense of earnestness or urgency that was common after the war?

LH: I think it's different. At that time men were drafted, people lived on rations, and the entire world was at odds. On top of that, memories of the Great Depression still loomed. Everyone was looking for the rainbow in the sky. We need this now, in some ways more than ever. I think there's more distraction in modern times though (sometimes good, sometimes bad) that changes the mood.

AM: This is, as I've said, your first novel. Where were you when you first decided to write it?

LH: I was at home listening to music. A band called The Civil Wars used to do this really cool "folky" music and something about it conjured up my vision of Jimmi-Lyn. Once I had her character I thought she'd fit well in a tiny town in the middle of nowhere I'd once driven through with my husband. Sydra came out of thin air sometime before that, and then I realized she was Jimmi-Lyn's sister. And just like that, they started talking to me.

AM: Fascinating. As they spoke to you, did you ever try to plug up your ears, refusing to listen and resisting the direction they wanted to take, or did their qualities and characteristics materialize naturally? I guess I'm asking if you told the story as you set out to tell it, or if the book took on its own shape unexpectedly.

LH: I always have a loose blueprint, but as I become my characters, it always changes somewhat. I think it helps make dynamic characters though. I envisioned Sydra a villain, but then I started rooting for her. It seems outside my own imagination at times. They do what they like. I'm just the girl typing.

AM: Well I hope you keep on typing. I look forward to seeing more of your work.

Idabel Allen

AM: The title of your book is *Rooted*. The first line signals that this word, *rooted*, will take on layers of meaning. "It all comes from the root," your narrator says. "And Grover McQuiston was the root of it all." What are you after here?

IA: The opening line of *Rooted* serves a couple of purposes. As there are three distinct voices or narratives—Grover, Slade, and Sarah Jane—the opening line is a way of tying these elements of the story together. Feedback for *Rooted* encouraged me to write the story from one voice, not three. I'd tried that in earlier drafts and the story never quite came together until I developed the three narratives. "It all comes from the root" is something my son told my grandmother a few years earlier. When trying to think of a way to address workshop feedback, this line came back to me, and I knew it was exactly what was needed to tie the narratives together.

The opening line also informs the reader up front that everything to follow in the story had an origin and that origin is the patriarch of a powerful Southern family. Also, it indicates a deep, family story line with a strong connection to the land. *Rooted* is very much a regional story, specific to the Delta. The earth and crops and fields and river are all important to the story and the characters. They draw comfort from their surroundings and feel a deep sense of belonging on that plot of land more so than anywhere else.

Finally, I wanted there to be a sense that no matter where you go, the roots that bind you to a people and place never go away. We are always rooted to our families and our past and our histories. And, moreover, we are responsible for the health and growth of our own roots, and their offshoots.

AM: Fascinating that your inspiration for that line came from your son—and fitting, too, given that roots and family are so important to the narrative. Where are your own roots?

IA: My roots run deepest in the West Tennessee Delta—from Memphis in the southwest corner of the state all the way up to Union City, the northwest corner where *Rooted* is set. On my father's side, family reunions filled with plates of fried catfish, country ham, hush puppies and baked apples were held at Reelfoot Lake in this same area. My grandparents owned and still own a small farm where we children rode in the combine, the harvested soybeans raining down on us like pennies from heaven.

My mother's family followed an almost migratory path, from Memphis to California to Memphis and back; rolling along on Elvis, Memphis Soul and the sixties sounds emerging from the San Francisco area: Janis and Jefferson Airplane and more.

My mother's love of music carried over to her children. Just as my father's strong connection to the land laid the foundation from which we operate. It is safe to say, *I'm a little bit country and a little bit rock n' roll.* And I think that comes across in *Rooted.*

Then there's a part of me that was influenced by the few years spent in Portland, Oregon, in middle school. Paper drives and field trips to the symphony and environmental camps were all new experiences that I took to and appreciated. In Portland, I realized that I would write books, and not just any books, but good books like the ones I devoured as a child—*Captains Courageous, Dr. Zhivago, East of Eden,* and anything by Ray Bradbury.

And that is what I am—a writer of books, drawing on the experiences and relationships and places that formed my youth.

AM: Reading, of course, is one of those experiences, and you mentioned some books you read during childhood. Are there particular writers who've informed or shaped your writing style?

IA: When I began writing *Rooted*, I was heavily into William Faulkner, Eudora Welty and Truman Capote. Rereading *Rooted*, I'm struck by elements similar to Faulkner's *Sartoris*—the patriarch, banker grandfather, the return of wild-child grandson, even the feisty old aunt. I wasn't consciously aware of the influence *Sartoris* had on my book when writing, but it supports the old saying "imitation is the sincerest form of flattery."

My writing has been compared to that of Flannery O'Connor, a writer I greatly admire but came to know later in life after *Rooted* was completed. Other writers who have had an impact on my work include John Steinbeck, Charles Portis, Ray Bradbury, Toni Morrison, Zora Neale Hurston, Virginia Woolf, Anton Chekhov, Jane Austen, Willa Cather and Cormac McCarthy.

Recently, I undertook Fyodor Dostoevsky's *Crime and Punishment* and *The Brothers Karamazov* and intend to do a deeper dive of his work.

My favorite book is John Kennedy Toole's *Confederacy of Dunces*. I have a soft spot for lovable losers like Ignatius J. Reilly, Portis' Ray Midge in *Dog of the South*, and characters in Steinbeck's *Tortilla Flat* and *Cannery Row*.

AM: When you say "deeper dive," do you mean you hope to study Dostoevsky or experiment with his influence in your fiction?

IA: I mean to read Dostoevsky's other books for enjoyment and to also better understand what he was trying to say through his fiction. Much of what he wrote about in *The Brothers Karamazov* in regards to this turn from religion towards science, or man's autonomy, and resulting isolation is very much a foreshadowing of the world we live in today—politically and socially.

I don't know that I would knowingly try to experiment with his influence in my fiction. But I certainly hope that his work would influence my fiction in a more natural, organic way. That is how it seems to work with me. I sponge up what I read, and then what I read seeps out onto my pages without any formal plan on my part.

AM: When did words start seeping onto the pages of *Rooted*?

IA: They started seeping in the late nineties. I was completing a novel, my first but one I will never do anything with, when I started thinking about a character "stuck" in a small, West Tennessee cotton town in the late 1970s. I say "stuck" because there's not a whole lot going on in such a place and time. And if you weren't born there, I don't know that you'd appreciate the people or the culture. This character originally had a broken leg and no way to leave town.

It wasn't long before the character grew into a New York punk rocker, Slade Mortimer. With a nasty habit and nasty attitude, he is on the run from his dead girlfriend's revenge-seeking father. For the residents of Moonsock, Slade might as well have come from outer space, so foreign was he to all they hold dear.

When *Rooted* first seeped into my conscious and ultimately onto the page, I also had in mind a young woman who had a hard time connecting with people. This character was to work at the funeral home as a beautician. Her specialty was making women corpses up to look like country music stars: Dottie West, Loretta Lynn, Tammy Wynette and Dolly, of course. This line of work did not make it into *Rooted*, as Sarah Jane developed into a darker, more damaged character.

From these two characters the plot developed and the story took on a life of its own. Between starts and stops and kids and jobs and other writing, I didn't finish *Rooted* until 2010. From there the book was with an agent in New York while I plugged away at another novel, *Strange Agonies In Some Lonesome Wilderness*.

AM: And is this other novel still in the works?

IA: *Strange Agonies In Some Lonesome Wilderness* is basically complete, or at least I thought it was until reading reviews of *Rooted*. Many people have remarked how easy *Rooted* is to read. This feedback has made me realize how much readers appreciate a story that is not cumbersome or difficult to get through.

Strange Agonies is a historical novel covering many periods: slavery, Reconstruction, and the Great Depression. There's a great deal of hoodoo in the story and history of Natchez, Mississippi, and surrounding areas. It is by far the most complex book I've undertaken, and I want to make sure that the complexity of the story does not interfere with readability. To ensure the book is as enjoyable and easy to read as *Rooted*, I am taking another pass through the manuscript and removing or revising anything that may cause a reader to pause or to be uncertain about what they are reading.

Once this review is completed, the book will be ready to publish. I haven't decided on a release date, but believe *Strange Agonies* will be in stores by Christmas or sometime soon after.

AM: Well congratulations on the big push toward publication. Looking forward to reading this next book.

Emily Carpenter

AM: *The Weight of Lies* is a thriller that critics have labeled as "Southern Gothic." Are they right?

EC: I wholeheartedly endorse the Southern Gothic label. There are some other elements at play in the book—bits of romance, horror, and family drama—but overall, I'd really hoped for that delicious moss-draped, muddy, "there's-something-off-about-this-place" feel you get in the best Southern Gothic books. The bulk of the novel takes place on a private island off the coast of Georgia. Throw in a mysterious, unsolved murder, and, frankly, it doesn't get more Southern Gothic than that.

AM: And you live in Georgia?

EC: I do. I am from Alabama and went to Auburn University, but have—for the most part—lived in Georgia since the 90s. I've had the good fortune to vacation on Sea Island, St. Simons and explore several of the other smaller islands off the coast, and they provided the inspiration for Bonny, the fictitious island in the book.

AM: War Eagle! I live in Auburn and earned my doctorate there. Do you ever make it back?

EC: I do occasionally. I love Auburn—have great memories there. I miss it. War Eagle!

AM: Central to *The Weight of Lies* is book-within-a-book framing: Your characters write or have written books. How did you come up with this approach?

EC: It's a job I know, obviously, being a writer, and so can speak with a little bit of authority on it. Which means I didn't have to do a whole lot of research.

But seriously, the book-within-a-book structure is definitely not an idea I came up with. Other books have done it—one I'm thinking of in particular is Rainbow Rowell's *Fangirl*.

I didn't necessarily set out to handle it like she did, with the brief excerpts of the book inserted every other chapter, but as the novel evolved, I discovered that approach seemed to work for the narrative and injected a lot more tension and suspense into what was going on, so I did end up doing it.

I was fascinated that this young woman Meg could've grown up with such a wildly famous novelist mother—basically her whole life was shaped by the success of one book—and she had never managed to read it. I think that said a lot about who she was as a person, how she had dealt with things in her life. And so this is the turning point where she's finally going to just read the damn thing, see what all the fuss is about and decide for herself if her mother is a hero or villain or something in between.

AM: You mentioned Rainbow Rowell. What other contemporary authors do you enjoy reading?

EC: Stephen King, Neil Gaiman, Philippa Gregory, Gillian Flynn, Jo Jo Moyes, Joshilyn Jackson, Paula Hawkins. As you can see I'm all over the map in terms of genre.

AM: Do you have a favorite genre—as a reader, not as a writer?

EC: I really do love suspense, which is why I decided to write it. It's my go-to genre. It all started with Nancy Drew probably. I used to pretend I was her when I was a little girl, only my neighborhood was disappointingly lacking when it came to mysteries that needed solving by a ten-year-old.

AM: Interesting how the person we are as children turns out to be so like the person we are as adults, no matter how much we protest or attempt to change our likes and preferences. Did you write as a child?

EC: I read mostly, voraciously. I attempted a few stories, but because creative writing wasn't really a part of the school curriculum, I don't think I realized it was something a kid could do. And I didn't really understand how to go about it. Isn't that strange? It was like I needed to be given permission to do it.

The first time I remember a teacher actually assigning us a creative writing exercise I was in junior high and I wrote this descriptive paragraph. The teacher read mine out loud and complimented it and it was like a life-changing experience for me, being told I was good at something. I've never forgotten it. Never forgotten how special that teacher, Mrs. Flowers, made me feel.

AM: Were there others who helped to cultivate your facility with the written word?

EC: Not really. During college, I did dabble in writing for the school newspaper, and at one point, I had an English professor suggest I major in English because he thought my essays were good. But for the most part, what little writing I attempted, I kept under wraps.

After college, I tried my hand at screenwriting, which wasn't really taught anywhere near me, so reading craft books was pretty much the extent of my training. I've never taken a fiction-writing class—except one weeklong workshop two years ago from Benjamin Percy, which was fantastic. Craft books have been a lifeline.

AM: Do you ever teach writing?

EC: I don't really consider myself a teacher, but maybe one day. I could probably see myself getting into a week-long workshop format. I probably have about a week's worth of helpful information to share with folks. I did start a writing accountability program called *The Draft House* with another author M.J. Pullen where we help people reach word counts and finish a first draft of their novels.

AM: How strict was your writing schedule for *The Weight of Lies*?

EC: I drive myself fairly hard when I'm drafting a book. For *Weight* I made myself write 1,000 – 2,000 words a day, not including weekends.

These days I'm a little more forgiving because I've realized I can't always forge ahead if the story isn't there yet. Sometimes it's more productive to allow myself that thinking time, in order to settle on just the way I want to write a scene.

The only problem with me is, I'm no good at skipping ahead to write another scene. I'm so linear, to a weird degree. I feel as if each scene builds on the last, not only in terms of plot, but tension. So that slows me down at times.

AM: Has your linear mode of thinking led to any new book ideas?

EC: So, I should clarify: I'm super-linear when I'm drafting a new book, but I'm all over the map when it comes to new ideas. Sometimes I'll think up a hook or it'll just be a scene, character or even a climactic moment. New ideas do not respect my need for order.

AM: Thanks, Emily, for taking the time to discuss *The Weight of Lies* and your writing.

EC: Thank you! Great chatting with you.

JESSICA HOOTEN WILSON

AM: You've written three books in quick succession that should appeal to readers of *Southern Literary Review*. The first involves Flannery O'Connor, and the second and third, Walker Percy. I'd like to start by asking about the second book, *Walker Percy, Fyodor Dostoevsky, and the Search for Influence*, because I'm also interested in notions of influence. Read my book on Holmes if you don't believe me. What distinguishes your treatment of influence from, say, Harold Bloom's, and what are your central claims about Dostoevsky's influence on Percy?

JHW: I take Harold Bloom to task in my book, both in my introduction and more explicitly in my conclusion, which is titled "A Christian's Response to Harold Bloom's *The Anxiety of Influence*."

Despite Bloom's genius, I audaciously argue that he misunderstands Christianity and thus influence as it functions in the Christian tradition. Bloom argues that the Protestant God places its followers in a double bind of "Be like Me" but "Do not presume to be too like me." The premise of his influence theory is profoundly religious, but the correct interpretation of the Protestant—or I would be more ecumenical and say Christian—God is a command to follow me down a path of kenosis, which is self-emptying. If one follows a leader into such great humility, then there is no rivaling.

Medieval writers understood this path for centuries—they all glossed the old stories without feeling a desire to overcome them or outdo them with individual originality. Marie de France claims in her prologue that she retells ancient stories to help her readers in building their characters and developing virtue. Chaucer saw the value of Dante and Boccaccio and he purposefully reset the good and true of their stories in his time and place, as did Shakespeare after him.

I claim that Percy, after he converted to Catholicism, recognized how writers before him had imitated other Christian authors in order to tell the best stories and perpetuate the good, true, and beautiful. He had no idea how to be a writer, and especially how to write for a secular audience about the truths he discovered in his faith. But, as he tells Caroline Gordon, he thought Dostoevsky most succeeded in such a venture, in writing Christian novels that could do "ass-kicking for Jesus," as Percy says. So, he copied him—aesthetically, in content, and in theme. Yet, without any of the rivaling or need for originality that Bloom claims exists.

AM: What first drew you to Percy?

JHW: There's the real answer, then there's the answer that makes a good story and will make others want to read Percy.

The first is that Percy was forced upon me in various situations—graduate seminars, mostly. I thought he was a good storyteller, but it was not love at first read. I didn't get what he was up to, and there were too many middle-aged men having frivolous affairs with young girls.

However, my relationship with Percy began when I investigated his papers housed at the University of North Carolina at Chapel-Hill. Suddenly I found a kindred spirit: I read his teaching notes on Dostoevsky's *Notes from Underground* and his reading notes on *The Idiot*. I read his letters and manuscripts. Getting inside his work, I discovered his vision and philosophy. Suddenly I could read the novels with different eyes. What I hoped to have done in my two books on Percy is to give readers those eyes, that they may have more of my second reading experience than my first.

AM: What's your focus in your forthcoming book on Percy, the guide to his novels?

JHW: The offer to write the book came from Margaret Lovecraft, an editor at LSU press. It was her idea! We met at the St. Francisville Walker Percy Festival where I've met hundreds of autodidact followers of Percy. The goal of the book is to make Percy's philosophy accessible. Percy claimed to be putting great ideas into story form. I go through each of his novels and distill the philosophy from the narrative. Vocationally, I'm a teacher at heart. As I wrote the guide to Percy's novels, I imagined before me the faces of my students and friends of mine who do not possess the storehouse of canonical thinkers to locate Percy's use of Kierkegaard or Augustine. The book is a reader's guide, not a scholar's guide; it introduces Percy's ideas primarily through close reading.

AM: You're also a scholar of Flannery O'Connor.

JHW: I am. I fell for Flannery when I was fifteen. A professor at Rhodes College told me my short stories sounded like PBS sitcoms. As an antidote, he gave me "The Life You Save May Be Your Own." From then on I was hooked. I wrote my first book on O'Connor's connections to Dostoyevsky and I teach her short stories in every class where I can get away with it.

AM: Do you have a favorite O'Connor story?

JHW: "Greenleaf" is one of my favorites because I love holy fools like Mrs. Greenleaf. Mrs. May's response to her is perfect, "Jesus would be ashamed of you!" Her inability to see herself and others clearly is unparalleled; it rivals even the blindness of Mrs. McIntyre or Mrs. Turpin. Also, the story is rich with classical allusion, such as Jove and Europa, as well as Christian allusion, the "uncouth country suitor" as a Southern description of Christ the loving pursuer. Then, that ending with Mrs. May gored through the heart and pulled down into unbearable light is beautiful.

AM: Your book on O'Connor and Dostoevsky is titled *Giving the Devil His Due*. These authors are separated by a wide gap in time and space, yet you pair them together to explore Christian themes. What is their connection? Why consider them with and against each other?

JHW: Funnily enough, I recently presented at the Walker Percy Festival where I met a Russian immigrant who told me that her discovery of Southern literature was the first time she felt at home over here! It's a pretty common comparison anecdotally but not scholarly.

Originally, the discussion was superficial: both the U.S. and Russia abolished slavery rather late on the world stage and at the same times; both regions were always being compared to their neighbors (for the South, it was that overbearing North whereas for Russia, it was the European continent). However, further inquiry showed me connections in their work that helped me better understand what was true about their stories, what correlated with reality in both their content and styles. They both are investigating the death of God in their society and how it correlates with a rise of autonomous individualism.

Many of my ideas come from my teachers. I then synthesized and elaborated upon what they taught me. It was hard in writing the book to distinguish my own ideas from these looming academic geniuses because without them, I would have no knowledge of the text. I was fortunate to study both O'Connor and Dostoevsky under top scholars—Ralph Wood taught me both; Paul Contino introduced me to Dostoevsky; and Louise Cowan taught me both Southern literature and Russian literature.

AM: And now you're teaching students of your own, passing along that inherited wisdom. Do you enjoy teaching?

JHW: I know exactly who I am and who I was meant to be in a classroom. My first teaching experience was teaching fourth grade at a classical school in Fort Worth, Texas. I experienced such confidence in my vocation in that first job. When I began teaching high school the next year, I realized how much I needed to learn to teach them well. Hence, graduate school. However, in graduate school, it was hard to remind myself that I was building up the storehouse of knowledge to be given away later. After all, I was there mostly to fill my tank and train my soul for teaching. Now, when I'm in the classroom, I light up like a firecracker when my students engage in conversation. We celebrate every discovery in the text, and I immediately call my husband after each class and ramble delightedly, debriefing that day's teaching. Long answer to say yes, I love teaching.

AM: And I'm confident our readers will learn from your books as well. Thank you for this interview, Jessica. I've enjoyed it.

Amber D. Tran

AM: So glad for the opportunity to talk to you about your debut novel, *Moon River*. Before we get into the book, I want to ask about your background. I noticed you're a graduate of West Virginia University. I studied English for my master's at WVU and graduated from law school at WVU. Did you study in the English department there?

AT: I did. I actually spent my first two years of college at a smaller school, West Liberty University, before transferring to West Virginia University. I did this because I was terrified about having required classes with more than 200 students. I spent my first two years at WLU, my last two years at WVU, and ultimately received a bachelor's degree in English literature with a concentration in creative writing from WVU in 2012. When I visit West Virginia, I try my best to return to the campus and speak with some of my professors. They were some of the most talented individuals I have ever met.

AM: Which professors, specifically?

AT: Kevin Oderman, Mark Brazaitis, Jim Harms, Mary Ann Samyn, and Amanda Leigh Cobb.

AM: I never had courses with them, but I heard good things. I take it that you learned your craft from them, in no small degree. Although you began writing at a very young age, no?

AT: That is correct. I've been writing since I was in the 5th grade. Throughout middle school and high school, I made sure my craft stayed active, even if I produced junk. It was during college, however, underneath the watchful eyes of my professors that I learned to polish my work and transform it into worthy pieces of literature. I owe them so much. To this day I use their advice in my writing. For example, for poetry, Mary Ann taught me the importance of the line; I make sure to hear her voice every time I write a new poem.

AM: And here you are now with your first novel under your belt. What should our readers know about this novel?

AT: Readers should know that this is a work of fiction inspired by true events. Readers are safe to assume that I inspire a lot of characteristics and behaviors of the protagonist, Abigail. This novel takes place in northern West Virginia and follows the friendship between two children, Abigail and Ryan, as they grow into adolescence and learn how to fit in as kids, preteens, and teenagers. A lot of heart and home exists in this book, that's for sure!

AM: Have you always written about heart and home?

AT: For the most part, yes. I am in awe of where I was born and raised. There is something special about West Virginia. A lot of my work is inspired by Appalachia. I have tried writing about other things, like science fiction and joy, but the inspiration is not as powerful. I'm a homely writer who likes to focus on the troubling and bleak. Perhaps it just makes for better literature.

AM: And now you live in Alabama, as do I. Do you think this move will affect what and how you write?

AT: Definitely not. My roots are in West Virginia. A part of the state is with me always. However, I will say that, for whatever reason, I've been meaning to write about a bed and breakfast in the Alabama area. This has been an idea of mine for a while. If I ever find the time to research the idea more, and if I muster the courage to steer away from West Virginia, I may give that idea a chance.

AM: Who are your favorite writers?

AT: Jo Ann Beard, Kerry Cohen, Kelly Braffet, Amanda Boyden, R. A. Nelson, and Jennifer Armintrout.

AM: What do you do when you aren't writing?

AT: When I'm not writing, I am trying to read. Sometimes other tasks get in the way, such as house cleaning and dog sitting. My husband and I love to play video games together, such as *League of Legends, Tera,* and *Overwatch.* We have spent many hours on our computers duking it out with friends

AM: Even though you wrote it, did you read *Moon River* when you first received your published copy in the mail?

AT: I did! I pulled out the very first copy from the printer's box and began reading. I had tears in my eyes. Some dropped onto the first few pages. It amazed me that I could hold four years of work in my hands. The experience was an emotional one.

AM: I hope our readers will have the same experience. Thanks for doing this interview, Amber.

AT: Thank you for having me! I appreciate the time you have spent with me.

Katherine Clark

AM: I'm only now reading *The Harvard Bride*, which I somehow missed upon its release, and now we're on the verge of the publication of *The Ex-Suicide*. I'd like to talk to you about both books.

KC: Don't forget *The Headmaster's Darlings* and *All the Governor's Men,* the first two novels in the Mountain Brook series.

AM: You're an Alabama native; I'm an Alabama transplant. I'm curious about your depiction of Mountain Brook in *The Harvard Bride*. It seems similar to the suburb of Atlanta where I grew up—a place where "money and status were magical forces which conferred complete protection on those who possessed them." To what extent did you set out to critique certain social conventions in this area, and to what extent were you merely describing?

KC: When I started writing the first novel in the series, I did not intend to write satirical fiction. But as soon as I started writing about Mountain Brook, what happened on the page was satire. Mountain Brook is one of those places that satirizes itself because it's so over-the-top in many ways. Simply observing or describing the reality of life in Mountain Brook is enough to create satire.

AM: The character Daniel is quickly and eminently recognizable, at least for those of us who spend time around lawyers. But Caroline is a more complex case. She's bookish and curious and a product of the very environment she now resists. Did you find yourself trying to work through tensions in her personality, or did you try to let those tensions hang there suspended, as we all hold onto competing impulses and desires and habits of thinking?

KC: My mission with the Caroline character was to recreate the tensions or inner conflicts that exist in a person who has a love/hate relationship with her hometown. It's the dilemma William Faulkner made famous with his Quentin Compson character, especially when he declares: "I don't hate the South! I don't hate it!" The reader knows from this vehemence and defensiveness that Quentin both does and does not hate the South. Characters who are at war within themselves make for interesting reading.

AM: Caroline goes off to Harvard to study and then returns home a different person. You did something similar, no?

KC: I did go to Harvard and sure, it changed this Alabama girl. But I never returned home afterwards to live in Birmingham. While there are several autobiographical parallels between myself and the Caroline character, much of her story in the novel is the product of imagination.

AM: I'm curious about your transition from university professor to professional novelist. How did that come about?

KC: I've wanted to write fiction since I read my first work of fiction in first grade. So I've had a long apprenticeship. I got a Ph.D. and became a professor so I could support myself while trying to write novels. Then eight years after I got married, my husband needed to move for his job, and I was unable to find a teaching position in our new location. So I concentrated full time on writing, treated this as my new job, and the Mountain Brook novel series is the result.

AM: When I first heard in 2016 that Pat Conroy had died, I immediately tweeted the news alerts, tributes, and obituaries. I was shocked. One of my first thoughts was, *what's going to happen to Story River Books*? For readers' sakes, I'll mention quickly that Conroy was the editor-at-large of Story River Books, an imprint of the University of South Carolina Press. It appears, to me, that the press is pushing forward. What's the editorial process like without Conroy?

And, if I may, what was it like with him?

KC: I don't know what the editorial process is like without Pat, since he read all four Mountain Brook novels and discussed them with me through and through several years before he passed away. He also gave me an idea for a fifth Mountain Brook novel, which I'm still pondering. He wanted me to continue with the Nick and Caroline characters from *The Harvard Bride*, and gave me a great idea for a plot. If I try to pull that off, then I'll experience what the editorial process is like without Pat Conroy.

Here's what was so great about Pat as an editor: He was a passionate cheerleader, full of praise and enthusiasm for his authors. When he was in the middle of reading my manuscripts, he would call me up in the middle of the day to laugh or exclaim about something I'd written. Can you think of anything more gratifying or encouraging for an emerging author?

His respect for my work built my confidence as a writer to a level I would not have reached without him. Then, when he slipped in a suggestion, a question or a criticism, my confidence was so solid that I could consider the critique and act on it without losing faith in my efforts. He treated me as an equal—as a writer with ability equal to his—which is not the case, but the dynamic he created by treating me that way has helped spur me to keep on writing and get better at it.

AM: An Al.com article once called you a "protégé" of Conroy. Is that the right term?

KC: If a protégé is someone who is supported and guided by an older and more accomplished mentor, then absolutely I was a protégé of Pat Conroy's.

I was not young when I first met him, so it cannot be said that he mentored me through my coming of age or my coming to consciousness. On the other hand, I was an unpublished novelist with 2½ manuscripts I didn't know what to do with when I first met him.

Pat guided and supported me through the process of making those manuscripts the best they could be, and then told me he wanted to publish them under his imprint Story River Books. This gave me the courage to finish the third novel and also write a fourth. Then Pat started talking about a fifth, and even began helping me hatch a plot for it.

AM: *The Ex-Suicide* is about to come out, and may in fact come out by the time this interview reaches publication. What's this book about?

KC: *The Ex-Suicide* is about a family living in the house across from the Birmingham Country Club that was once occupied by the writer Walker Percy, who coined the term "ex-suicide." This is my most ambitious Mountain Brook novel thus far, because it attempts to engage with the legacy of Birmingham's racial past.

AM: Should we expect to see some of the same Mountain Brook characters we've come to know from your other books?

KC: Yes, this novel focuses on characters who have been on the sidelines in other Mountain Brook novels. And of course Norman Laney makes his appearance as well.

AM: Thanks for the interview, Katherine. I look forward to reading *The Ex-Suicide*.

KC: Thank you, Allen.

Bren McClain

AM: Thanks for the interview, Bren. Before we talk about your new book, *One Good Mama Bone*, I'd like to mention something we have in common: We both studied English at Furman University. Who were your professors there?

BM: Dr. Stanley Crowe was my adviser. Also Dr. Pate, Gil Allen and Ann Sharp. Loved them.

AM: I took courses with Dr. Crowe and Dr. Pate and Dr. Allen as well. And I loved them too. They each had a tremendous influence on me as a student of literature and as a person. I miss them and Greenville. It's a beautiful town. Did you grow up in South Carolina?

BM: Yes, I grew up in Anderson, in a farming community west of town, where there were no subdivisions, only acres and acres of pastureland and cotton and wheat and oats. A girl could run free.

AM: What's your fondest childhood memory?

BM: I was in the sixth grade and at my grandmother's home across the road. She had a collie dog that was having puppies in a cramped dog house with lots of straw. I wanted to watch the birth, but my grandmother, Nana, thought it would be too much for me. "Please," I said, and she went for it. I sat up against the wooden wall across from the mama dog and watched in silence as her eyes bulged, her legs held out stiff like broom handles. She was in pain. Yet she welcomed into the world all six puppies, each one coated in a milky white sack; each one she gently licked off and nestled to her teats with her nose. I felt her love for them and began to cry. My grandmother came to check on me, saw my tears and wanted me to leave, thinking I was upset. "No," I told her, "I think it's beautiful." She let me stay. I think that's my fondest childhood memory, because it was the first real time I bonded with an animal and got a glimpse of how special they are. And also because my Nana let me stay.

AM: How does your sense of place find expression in your writing?

BM: Actually, I think my writing finds its expression in my sense of place. I grew up on a 72-acre beef cattle farm, and that environment has informed everything I write. The unadorned life of farmers, our dependence on, even subservience to, the weather and nature and the land. Not taking anything for granted. The importance of the church in the community and family and neighbors.

AM: Tell us about *One Good Mama Bone*.

BM: It's the story of Sarah Creamer, a dirt-poor woman who doesn't think she has a "mama bone," but is thrust into that world to take care of her husband's illegitimate son, after he can't live with what he's done and drinks himself to death. How will she survive? What I think sets the book apart is the form Sarah's "help" arrives in, a mama cow that comes to live on her farm and teaches Sarah how to be a mother. It's set in the early 1950s in rural South Carolina.

AM: I read an interview in which you were asked why you wrote about cows. Your answer was that you didn't choose the cows, the cows chose you. Explain what you meant.

BM: I was visiting my father's farm in late 2008, only to be awakened in the night by sounds that drew me outside to a gathering of mama cows, huddled in the corner of a barbed wire fence. I would come to know that their babies had been weaned from them the afternoon before. These mamas were calling for them, deep guttural calls, which seeped into my bones and made me think of my failed novel, an attempt to celebrate motherhood. But I had not pulled that off. There, in front of me, with these mama cows, lay the missing piece. I told them I couldn't bring their babies back, but I could tell their story. Guess who was in the center of that huddle? The cow I would name Mama Red! I made her a promise, bought her from my father and gave her forever sanctuary.

AM: You're on a big tour. What's that like?

BM: I begin tomorrow. But I'll go ahead now and tell you what it's like, because I know. It's like having weeks and weeks of celebration, as I get to connect with readers and booksellers. For me, connection, establishing relationships, is what it's all about. I embrace the days and nights ahead.

AM: Do you have a writing ritual?

BM: Yes. I'm a morning writer. I get up at 3:30, make a cup of coffee and go into my writing sanctuary beneath a stairwell and sit at my desk, which is a small organ from the 1800s that's been gutted. I write in the dark, save for the light from my laptop screen.

AM: How did you decide to play with different points of view in the novel?

BM: The story was bigger than any one person. Any attempt I made to isolate the narration to Sarah, my main character, fell woefully short. I wanted the reader to really get to know the other characters, their inner workings, what they loved, what they feared. It was a tall mountain to climb, let me say, but, oh so worth it. As I was rotating their points of view, I always asked myself – Where should the camera go now?

AM: Thanks for the interview, Bren.

BM: My pleasure, Allen. My absolute pleasure.

DANNY JOHNSON

APM: Congratulations on your debut novel, *The Last Road Home*. What's this book about?

DJ: The book is about discovery. Two kids, Junebug who is a white orphaned farm boy, and Fancy who is the daughter of black sharecroppers, meet and form a bond at the age of eight. They spend their growing-up years discovering the soul beneath their skin is very much the same. The relationship reveals Fancy's vision of a future void of hope and happiness simply because she is black, an image common among African Americans, and something Junebug never before considered. What they were as children changes when they come of age, a change which they discover has overwhelming odds. My objective was not to preach viewpoints, but, in the form of a delightful story, my hope is readers will have their own "aha" moments and come to conclusions about their own vision of life, while at the same time understanding it may not be one shared by other folks. The beauty of life is in our differences, not our similarities, and if Americans can "discover" and appreciate that simple concept, it will be a big step forward in the reconciliation of our country.

APM: Did you find it difficult to write about race relations in the 1960s South? Did you worry that this time and place had been thoroughly explored already, or were you convinced you could bring a fresh perspective?

DJ: I wasn't sure I could bring a completely fresh perspective, but I was sure I could bring a fresh story. I don't believe it possible to overstate what conditions a large segment of our population were forced to endure for so many years; therefore, we as writers have an obligation to be the voice of what we see. Someone pointed out recently that so many new books involving race were either out or coming out, and my response was: "that's great, how are we ever going to solve these issues if we can't talk about them." I have long held strong feelings about the racial disparity in America, and have spent years thinking about how the white population could in good conscience subjugate the black one, then poke out our chest to the rest of the world and declare ourselves "the land of the free."

My grandmother was the wife of a farmer, and spent her life digging in the dirt beside my grandfather in order to survive. What was different about my grandmother was she was born in 1903, graduated from high school and then taught school for a few years, this in a period when the normal rural community education was limited to anywhere from two years to six. I point this out only to say my grandmother had a different viewpoint on things about which she seldom spoke, one being I never heard her use the "N" word to refer to black folks. I asked her about it, because it was as common as "pass the biscuits" in my family. She told me it was a word poor white folks needed as a safety net; that it let them believe there would always be somebody less than them; that a white man could be a sot, beat his wife, etc., but as long as he could say "at least I ain't a N" he still had worth. When I began to write the story, her words kept coming back to me. I had two wonderful characters who ended up in a place I knew about and people I understood. What began as a story of friendship expanded, and allowed me to address the issues and values of that period and how I saw them change inch by inch. Our racial disparity began in the south, and I really believe it will be the south that brings us out of it. One has only to look around, listen, and read what's coming from southern writers to have hope that a tremendous change is coming.

APM: Did you have certain literary precursors in mind when you conceived of this narrative?

DJ: Not to be blasphemous, but Huckleberry Finn. On its surface, *Huckleberry Finn* is a story about a boy and a slave floating down the river, but underneath, the book is an exploration of racism in that period. I have always admired Mark Twain's courage in exposing in 1885 the same thing we find ourselves still addressing 135 years later. I did not write my novel with Huck Finn in mind, but it is a similar concept since my book uses a white boy and African American girl on a comparable, albeit unplanned, journey of personal discovery, while making a statement about the conditions of racism in the period.

APM: Every novelist has a story about how his first novel came into existence. What's yours?

DJ: There was a point a few years ago when I had nothing going. I had started and discarded a couple of novels because I could not find the voice I wanted. So, I began to sit at my computer in the morning and just start typing the first words that came to mind and then tried to make little stories from them, hoping something would click. After a couple of weeks, the two main characters in the novel showed up. I had no idea what to do with them at first, but once I paired the two in a time period I knew and in a place I knew, the story began to reveal itself. Over the next three years, I became an observer of the relationship and actions between the characters and let them tell the story, and simply wrote what I saw. My goal was for all the characters to reveal what was at stake for each of them, from the unnerving oppression to which some were subjected to the horrors of a war that tore our country apart. At the same time, I desperately wanted to keep alive Junebug and Fancy's love for each other.

APM: What's your background?

DJ: I grew up in a low-income city housing project, and my grandparents owned a farm in the county. I spent each summer with my grandparents, so I knew what that environment looked like, tasted like, and sounded like. I also came to understand the conflict between the love white folks had for African Americans as individuals versus their hate for the race.

I went into the military in 1965 and Vietnam in 1968. The book is dedicated to my African American Warrior Brother, Dot Dorsey, who was killed on February 5, 1969, when his plane flew into a mountain in Laos. I discovered so many levels of my ignorance from our friendship. I am a Distinguished Flying Cross recipient.

APM: And when did you first start writing?

DJ: I wrote my first story at the age of 62.

APM: Do fiction and nonfiction overlap in any way in *The Last Road Home*?

DJ: The individuals in the story are complete fiction; however, the attitudes and circumstances, both in growing up on a farm and in the war, are mostly based on memories. I think in literary fiction, there is always a foundation of truth, an obligation to teach what the reader may not be familiar with, and to present new ideas for them to consider.

APM: You've been busy promoting your book at bookstores and libraries. Has the publicity been fun?

DJ: I have always loved meeting folks and making new friends, chatting with them both about my book and their backgrounds, trying to understand what they may or may not have liked about the novel; and I must say the book has been very well received. The only real talent I've ever had is an intuitive understanding of people and that's been a blessing. I seem to have an overload of empathy for almost any circumstances, since many times I've experienced them myself (e.g., my wife is a cancer survivor, I had a kid on drugs, I've been to war, etc.). That's a long way around answering the question, but yes, I've had a glorious time with the folks who come to the readings; the travel, however, is hard on an old man. I just don't know how Stephen King does it.

I recently had an opportunity to be a part of the Inaugural Carolinas WordFest in Charlotte, North Carolina, a wonderful expansive literary experience for folks from kids to adults in a variety of genres. I was on a panel with four other amazing writers like L. Lamar Wilson, who is a brilliant man and addresses so many aspects of American culture, as well as Jim Grimsley and Mary Alice Monroe, who has about every literary award presented and has written so many books it's crazy. She's still so young—I don't get it. The panel exposed the audience to a variety of viewpoints about what literature is doing and can do to address the racial and cultural divide in America, and it was wonderful to be included with folks of such high caliber.

APM: Thanks for this interview, Danny. I wish you much success.

Julia Nunnally Duncan

AM: Julia, it's great to have the opportunity to promote a regular contributor to *Southern Literary Review*. Tell us a little about your new collection of essays, *A Place That Was Home*.

JND: Thank you, Allen. I appreciate your introducing my new book to your readers.

A Place That Was Home is my first nonfiction book. For several years, I've been writing essays about my experiences here in Western North Carolina and was inspired to compile a book of personal essays after reading Flora Thompson's *Lark Rise to Candleford*. My book traces my life from around 1960 to the present day—my childhood, teenage years, and adulthood.

AM: This book required some research, did it not? People don't always associate research with the personal essay.

JND: Yes, the research was necessary for several of the essays, such as "Charlie's Knife." To better understand the central character—my great-uncle Charlie Lynch—I had to research his World War I service, initially based on certain details of his uniform that I noticed in an old family photograph. With the help of various Internet sites, mainly Ancestry.com, I discovered facts about him that few people in my family ever knew. For me, this discovery was like finding buried treasure and was deeply gratifying.

For the essay "A Place That Was Home," I wanted to learn as much as possible about a 1929 textile workers' strike that occurred in my hometown Marion, North Carolina. My mother's family lived in a cotton mill village during this time, so she experienced this textile strike firsthand and has talked about it for years. However, I needed to know what instigated the strike and learn more about its deadly consequences.

In general, I want to be accurate in my historical details. Research ensures this accuracy.

AM: The book's title comes from the title of this essay. It's a wistful essay involving family. There's so much packed into that one word, "was."

JND: Yes, there is much packed in that word, and I appreciate your perceiving this.

I used the word "was" versus "is" because in the collection's final essay, "A Place That Was Home," my mother visits a community that has not been her home for decades. Yet this place that "was" home during her childhood is still so deeply ingrained in her memories and dear to her heart that it will always in some way be her true home. She's never really left it. I think the word "was" evokes the past and emphasizes its importance.

AM: Do you have a favorite essay in the book?

JND: Probably "A Place That Was Home." This essay captures a past time and place in my hometown. It's also my way of preserving some entertaining moments from my mother's early life in a Great Depression-era cotton mill village, which had an interesting culture of its own.

AM: What's the most important thing for an aspiring essayist to learn?

JND: To realize that his or her experiences are indeed important and unusual enough to record. Every life is unique and each perspective different. Through recollecting and writing, I discovered that much drama and occasional strangeness have permeated my seemingly normal rural world.

AM: What's something you feel is unique or distinctive about your style?

JND: I do have a tendency to write about cemeteries, funeral homes, and quirky characters. These places and people have been part of my small-town Southern life, and I find them compelling.

AM: Place and home. These concepts are important to you. What, in your opinion, do they mean?

JND: I think that place, for better or worse, dictates a lot of what we are—our mannerisms, our voices, our attitudes. Some people spend their lives trying to erase the mark that a place has left on them, but in my writing I want to preserve my own place—its language, its landscapes, its history. And home suggests sanctuary to me. At the end of the day, home is where we go back to. For some, it can be visited only in memory. But whatever home is to a person, its importance is profound.

AM: Thanks so much for answering these questions, Julia. Congratulations on the publication of this book.

JND: Thanks again, Allen.

Deborah Mantella

AM: You're a transplant to the South. Yet the rich quality of your language is distinctly, authentically Southern. There's something Natasha Trethewey about it. You must be a reader of Southern literature.

DM: First of all, Allen, I am still trying to wrap my writer mind around your Natasha Tretheway reference. I am truly honored. I've always been a reader with eclectic taste, and to that end, I am constantly fine-tuning my own listening and monitoring skills. As any avid reader of literary fiction would likely attest, appropriately balanced, there is nothing quite like *Southern* to lend a lyricism, to enhance flavor. Place lends a special seasoning and in many instances is as important to story as character.

AM: Do you get nervous or anxious about getting your characters' dialect and colloquialisms just right?

DM: I do my best to set my world and then to let my characters take over. Their words are their words. As mentioned, serious listening is an important capability for any writer, second only to serious reading. When a reader opens a book a sacred bond is there for the making. I agonize over all details, dialect and colloquialisms included. It's part of the job. If I am going to ask you to follow me into this other universe, this cosmos I've created, it is my duty to get that world right.

AM: This is your first novel. At what point did you decide it needed to be written? What I mean is, when did you realize you had the makings of a book?

DM: At the outset, I wanted to see, hear, and feel the basic ideals of courage and righteousness, the best of the human spirit, jammed right up alongside the worst of humanity's shortcomings, frailties, and deceptions. In keeping with what happens in real life, I needed to allow time for Vidalia's own most intimate inner workings to catch up with what she'd gathered, by force, during her rough and tumble due diligence period.

I knew it was time once my narrator, the character of spirit-child Cieli Mae, was fully formed. With her impractical yet pragmatic presence, her otherworldly yet down-to-earth sensibilities, and her always nonsensical approach to what it means to be human, I couldn't wait to release her out into Vidalia's world.

AM: Where do you write?

DM: That's easy. Wherever I am when an idea strikes me—regardless of its condition. I may remember a concept, a notion, an insight, later on, but never in the same way. Once I've safely surrendered that concept, notion, or insight to a more concrete form, I can always improve upon it later.

AM: You've taught before. Did you teach writing?

DM: Writing is my personal default mode. As such, I find myself unable to exclude its intrinsic benefits, its finer points, the appreciation of language, of a sentence well-crafted, from the instruction of any subject, to any level of student. My father was my writing instructor. By profession he was an electrical engineer, but he should've been an English teacher. Or a writer.

AM: Do you believe writing is a craft that can be taught, or is it a natural gift—or something in between?

DM: I believe the *desire* to write is a gift. And that the *creativity* needed to assign order to a jumble of thoughts and words into a state of cohesiveness is also a gift. The capacity to turn that desire, that jumble, that coherency, to channel that creativity into a state of clarity is a craft whose mastery is both laborious and time-intensive.

AM: Could you talk about the importance of womanhood in *My Sweet Vidalia*? I'm referring to the concept, the trope, the metaphorical import.

DM: Womanhood rules the county of Willin, sets its parameters. Womanhood reigns supreme, whether or not its inhabitants yet know it, and even as any victory seems unlikely. The relationship between Vidalia and her spirit daughter and the addition of motherhood to the womanhood mix only ups the ante.

Despite gender-specific traits and situations, attributable at least in part to time and place, I prefer to consider my characters in terms of their own particular idiosyncrasies. And while there are several distinctly female heroes in this story—from the misguided to the hell-raising, from a feisty former suffragette to the honorable bearer of unfathomable burdens and to one soft-hearted enabler—who support one another when support is most needed, each is ultimately rescued, delivered from harm, by the vast potential of her own spirit.

AM: Thank you very much for the interview.

DM: Thank *you*, Allen.

Derek Furr

AM: Thanks for taking the time to answer a few questions about your new book, *Semitones*. I want to start by asking about the title. You provide an epigraph by John Dowland that works toward defining "semitones." Could you explain the significance of this title, which I'm guessing has to do with the unique musicality of your writing that is reflected, as well, by titles in the book: "Dawn Chorus," "Aubade" and "Aubade II," "Coda," "Kindertotenlieder," and "Evensong."

DF: Sound and music are important in all my work—sounds of the language and sentences, references to music. The idea for the title came to me when I was working on the prose pieces that are somewhat hard to define—lyric essay, prose poem, short poetic fiction? They are between recognizable keys, so to speak. Moving up or down a semitone, a melody also seems to be on its way somewhere, to be searching, unresolved.

AM: Why do you think there aren't more books like this one—books which combine poetry with the lyrical prose of short fiction.

DF: That is probably as much a matter of marketing as of art. Before I found Fomite, I had been told by more than one editor that my books needed to be all short fiction or all poetry. But that's not how I write, and it's too narrow a definition of "book." Historically, smaller presses have tended to welcome difference and push boundaries. Perhaps that's why some of the most important literary work of the 19th and 20th centuries began in tiny print runs and small publishing houses.

AM: Spirituality seems important in *Semitones*. I'm thinking of "The Annunciation of Mary of Upstate New York," mentions of God and Jesus and Buddha and the Virgin Mary, a prose poem—if that is the right classification—about Easter. Are you a spiritual person? A religious person?

DF: I was raised Baptist, and while I've moved far away from that doctrinally, I am still searching, because I still have faith that there is something to be found. It's always been important to me to understand the history and philosophy of religions, especially of the faith traditions that shaped me, and because I'm basically a student, I read about these matters whenever I can make time. I should probably also say that the language of the KJV, gospel songs, and hymns runs through my mind alongside that of the writers whom I've admired.

I do try to be disciplined about putting my mind on higher things—otherwise, they'll remain out of sight and mind. I play piano for a small, ethnically diverse and economically challenged Methodist congregation in the Hudson Valley. These are good people, many of whom have made mistakes or been dealt a bad hand, but they're trying to overcome. We do that in community, giving of ourselves. I guess what I'm describing is a ministry of social justice, which is what any religion or spirituality should be.

AM: Do you have a favorite poem or story or passage from the book?

DF: Recently I've been reading "Bruise" at my book signings. I have a deep affection for those characters and their pain. Also the idea of a "chorus of semitones."

AM: Am I right to detect the influence of modernist Americans like Wallace Stevens and Elizabeth Bishop, whose names appear in the book?

DF: Two of my favorites. I've written about Bishop, and I was rereading Stevens while I worked on several pieces from the book.

AM: How did you decide to include the sketches or illustrations by Andrés San Millán?

DF: Andrés is a friend—a generous spirit and talented performer and artist. Fomite encourages collaboration, and Andres was interested in trying to create drawings based on my work. At first, I was skeptical when he suggested drawing with the words themselves. But the results were so striking that I cannot now imagine the book without his drawings: the image for "Graveyard Encounters," for instance, or the way he depicted the threesome from "Become a Light."

AM: "The certain risk of a simple sentence." This phrase stuck with me, perhaps because some of your sentences are so powerful without being complex or ostentatious. I'm reminded of Richard Poirier's *Poetry and Pragmatism*, which attributed to certain modernists the ability to achieve "superfluity"—Poirier's loaded term—through the sounds of ordinary language employed with sensational effect.

DF: There is a bit of irony in the phrase, because I was experimenting with long sentences in that piece and others of its kind. In essence, that's what I do: work with sentences. Maybe that's what all writers do at some level.

AM: Death, ghosts—explain their place and significance in the book.

DF: We are surrounded by a cloud of witnesses. They're in books and music, as well as memories and bird song. And I've never met anyone who wasn't haunted. It's just a matter of being aware of what haunts you, facing it, trying to understand it, and if possible, giving it a voice in a key that others can recognize, or at least hear.

AM: Thanks for the interview, Derek. I enjoyed it.

Glenn Arbery

AM: First of all, congratulations on the publication of your novel, *Bearings and Distances*. You've got deep roots in the South but haven't lived here in some time. Do you ever feel a sense of, pardon the term, alienation?

GA: Thank you. As for a sense of alienation, sure I've felt it, but less in Wyoming than in New England. Alienation is a funny thing to try to describe. I suppose at its root it's the sense of being the *other*, the one who doesn't fit into the world per se, like Raskolnikov up in his little coffin of a room during the white nights of Petersburg, that artificial and archetypally modern city.

Full-bore alienation like that is hard to sustain when you're the father of seven girls and one boy and now the grandfather of thirteen. But I have to say that the times I have felt less at home were during the sixteen years we were in New England rather than the twenty in Dallas (and I don't consider Dallas the South).

What was it about the Northeast? Despite having many very good friends there, I always felt like an outsider. I think it's like the experience Mowbray anticipates when Richard II exiles him: "My native English, now I must forego." I'm kidding, but not entirely. There's something in the very idioms of living in New England that I never "got" or wanted to get, whereas I always recover my native idioms of being—instantly, effortlessly—when I return to the South. Being in New England drove me deeper into my Southern identity. That's where I wrote this novel. Living in Wyoming, on the other hand, reminds me in many ways of being in the South. It's no accident that *The Virginian* is set here.

AM: You're a scholar of Southern literature. *Bearings and Distances* is not necessarily a regional book, but global, although it is, I submit, Southern literature. The opening pages jump from the Deep South to Italy and reveal a familiarity with African literature, to give just one quick example of the breadth involved. The book is both deep and wide in its themes and allusions—from Christian to classical. If forced to put a genre label on the book, what would you choose?

GA: I definitely think of it as a Southern novel. When I talk about genre per se, I'm influenced by my teacher and friend Louise Cowan, who draws her genre theory from Aristotle's four major kinds or types: comedy, tragedy, epic, and lyric. I think that in its depths my novel *wants* to be comic—not just funny, but Dantean and purgatorial. Yet it certainly contains an action that tends toward tragedy, especially in the sense of repetition and a Greek feeling of fate. Because of the 40 years that it encompasses in the main character's return to his Southern hometown, it also has an epic cast in a biblical sense.

Before the election in 2008, Obama made a point of comparing himself to Joshua, who takes the Israelites into the Promised Land after their forty years in the Wilderness. His allusion was of course to Martin Luther King and his "mountaintop" speech the night before his death forty years earlier in 1968. Set in the summer of 2009 and looking back to 1969, the novel tests the heady claim—many people felt it in 2008—that we've made it past the issues of race and guilt that haunt the national psyche.

AM: Your novel deals with racial tension, right down to the fact that its main character, Braxton Forrest, shares the last name of the notorious Confederate general. Did you feel a sense of trepidation at approaching this subject?

GA: If you don't feel some trepidation about approaching the matter of race, you're not paying attention. Chattel slavery was a kind of original curse that we've had to work out in our national history, and the effects of it, because of its visible heritage, will not go away in our lifetime and perhaps not in the lifetimes of our great-grandchildren. This is one of the most intractable problems of our lives as Americans, not because of race per se, but because of the associations with slavery. I have no desire to rewrite—to use your excellent word—the problems of this history. I think they will never be completely solved by legislation or reparations, but they will be overcome, as they have always been overcome on a personal level, by love and loyalty and trust and generosity.

AM: All the rage in Southern studies involves the "global South," which makes sense to some extent in our increasingly globalized world. How do you feel about this trend, and how do you think *Bearings and Distances* both implicates and challenges it?

GA: I once had a student whose mother came from Mauritius in the Indian Ocean. When this student read Faulkner—*Absalom, Absalom* and *Go Down, Moses* in particular—she said that these novels took her inside the world of her mother's childhood, because her mother's French colonial circumstances (the big house, the servants) had been so similar to those recounted in Faulkner's novels. I think there's a common experience deriving from Rome that the South has always shared with French, Spanish, and Portuguese Central and South America, including the Caribbean, though for a long time its prevailing Protestantism kept it from admitting an affinity with its brethren.

Garcia-Marquez certainly looked to Faulkner, as did Edouard Glissant and many others. In the century after the Civil War, the South was so caught up either in trying to be like the rest of the country (the complaint of the Fugitive-Agrarians) or in claiming the status of defeated Troy or in asserting a discreditable difference, particularly in matters of racial politics, that it didn't see those larger dimensions.

On the other hand, I wince a little at the very term "global South." Fashion so shamelessly dominates academic writing that I have a hard time taking very seriously anything that's "all the rage," as you put it. (One of the aspects of *Bearings and Distances* is satire of the contemporary academy, which deserves a Swift.) I did not consciously comment on the "global South" per se in the novel, but one of its characters, Hermia Watson, certainly welcomes such concerns. Her father, Braxton Forrest, would make fun of them.

AM: You have a deep respect for the South—its traditions, myths, literature, and culture. *Bearings and Distances* **is in a way an exploration of these themes, is it not?**

GA: Very much so. Since I first went to the University of Georgia in the 1970s, I've been steeped in the work of the Fugitive-Agrarians as part of my literary education in general. I read Ransom, Davidson, Tate, and Warren alongside Eliot and Stevens and Frost; I was discovering Faulkner, Welty, O'Connor, Gordon, and Percy after reading Borges, Garcia-Marquez, and Nabokov. Marion Montgomery directed my Master's thesis. At the University of Dallas, I studied with Louise Cowan and Mel Bradford. But growing up in the South predisposed me to Southern traditions long before I read anything other than the Hardy Boys and Tom Swift and Edgar Rice Burroughs' Tarzan novels. I'm probably in the last generation when it was still impossible not to "grow up hating Sherman," as Shreve says to Quentin in *Absalom, Absalom*.

AM: You make no attempt to rewrite biological and sexual givens in terms of fashionable theory divorced from science.

GA: Well, it never occurred to me. I have considerable difficulty with the idea of "rewriting biological and sexual givens." Those givens seem to me the source of anguish, yes, but also of wonder and gratitude—emotions I have felt daily with our Down syndrome daughter, who is now 28. If we're talking about the moral and intellectual improvement of which we're certainly capable, sure, but the kind of "rewriting" I think you mean comes out of a narrative of self-ownership that I find unfortunate and sometimes laughable. If we could bestow a single moment of *existence* upon ourselves, perhaps it would be creditable, but we live and breathe and have our being out of a mystery more than biological. "Givens" imply a Giver, and it seems to me more honest and certainly more rewarding to ponder the constitution of that given-ness than to assert too much for the will and to make the shallow claims of self-invention.

AM: Do you consider yourself a religious writer?

GA: Ever since I grew up in a Methodist Church in Middle Georgia, religion has been very much a part of my weekly experience. When I was a child, it was simply part of the reality of things for everybody I knew, despite all our irreverence and merry transgression. Even after I began to have serious doubts as a teenager, the sense of religion never left me, and I came back to it as I matured. I have been a practicing Roman Catholic since I was 26. But am I a religious writer? I don't think so. I certainly don't intend to write homiletically. Simply as a *writer*, I can say that religion is now and has always been one of the central dimensions of human life; it pervades Homer and Virgil, for example. It's part of our nature to idolize if not to worship, to act in ritual ways, so much so that even those who reject religion tend to find substitutes that they don't recognize as religious. But by and large the South remains consciously and deliberately religious. To treat religious realities in fiction—including concerns about salvation—seems to me completely natural for a novelist; it's mimetically accurate; it's both in keeping with the traditions out of which we come and a way of thinking about the prospects, personal and cultural, that lie before us.

AM: How did you discover Wiseblood Books? I'm intrigued by the work it's doing.

GA: A friend in Massachusetts first told me about Wiseblood Books, and I was immediately interested. As I've told the founder, Joshua Hren, I wish I had had the gumption at his age to do something similar. Wiseblood offers writers who take their faith seriously a platform but it insists on literary integrity and truthfulness with respect to the way people really are, in all their sin and self-deception and vulnerability to grace. The name, too, felt like an appeal. The first real literary paper I wrote was on Flannery O'Connor's *Wise Blood*—Enoch Emery with his little mummy and his gorilla suit, Haze Motes and his "Church without Christ."

AM: Do you prefer to write fiction or scholarship?

GA: Fiction, no question. I've been late coming to it, because my creative work in the past has been largely with poetry.

In the past decade or so, fiction has begun to call me more powerfully. I've never felt myself to be a scholar, I confess. I've never truly been a master of a body of material, though I suppose I come closest with some of the Southern writers. My sympathies have always been with Montaigne in this regard: I love to read, and my reading tends to follow my interests, and my interests have never been specialized.

AM: Have you always thought of yourself as a writer of fiction, or was your decision to write a novel something you came to through your studies of, say, Shakespeare and Homer and Dostoevsky and so on?

GA: I genuinely don't remember exactly when I decided to write *Bearings and Distances*. I'd been trying some short stories, then trying something longer that didn't take on form, and I incorporated some things into this novel when it suddenly took hold several years ago. But I can't say that I wrote it because of Homer and Shakespeare and Dostoevsky—or Aeschylus, or Dante or Virgil and so on. Since 1986, I've been privileged to teach in places that center on great books. These works are simply part of the way I see the world, the way I imagine things, as they have been for most educated men and women in the Western world for most of our history. Personally speaking, this novel comes more from a desire to come to terms with my Southern past in a larger American context than from any explicit desire to emulate my betters.

AM: Thank you for this interview and for this searching, complex novel.

GA: Thank you, in return, for your generous interest.

Russell Scott

AM: Thank you for the interview and congratulations on the publication of *The Hard Times*. This novel opens in Mississippi with an alarming scene involving a doctor—or doctors—and then brings us to Africa. You're a doctor in Mississippi who's traveled to Africa. What's going on here?

RS: I guess you write what you know; it makes it more real. Truth for the most part is stranger than fiction, so you have to adjust real life to make it more believable.

AM: How much research into places and world events did this book require?

RS: Well, quite a bit: the details of the mining restrictions, the Kimberly Process, U.N. diamond regulations, and the details of the period of the transition of the government of Namibia all took a lot of reading. The details of what is happening in Zimbabwe also took some time.

AM: I take it you never shot Cecil the Lion.

RS: No, I'm not so much of a hunter. I like to walk around and watch the animals. I understand the nature of consuming meat, so I tend to shoot things I plan to eat. That didn't work out so well with the zebra. I couldn't get over the whole horse aspect of things, and eating it was not that great an experience for me, but the locals love it and all of the meat was consumed.

AM: How do you find time to write and practice medicine, or are the two practices mutually illuminating?

RS: I think everything you do affects your writing. Being a physician is a part of who I am. You can't divorce any aspect of who you are from your writing and remain true to yourself as an author.

AM: China Grove Press is relatively new, correct?

RS: Yes, it is a new entity formed from two other entities, Magnolia Gazette Publishing—which has been in continuous operation since 1872, it's the oldest business in Pike County, Mississippi—and IsoLibris, a company designed to produce ebooks, which was only a couple of years old.

AM: What's the significance of the poem at the beginning of the book?

RS: It is a poem I wrote sitting on my back porch watching an approaching storm; it seemed to set the stage for the book, and the storms coming for everyone in it.

AM: Who is Ray Moffett? Is he a good person?

RS: He's my "everyman," trying to find a way back into grace from the transgressions of his life. So he's both good and bad, but mostly he's like the weeds in the poem, buffeted by the winds, or the particles of dust…moved by collisions he can neither avoid nor anticipate.

AM: You've got a lot of military experience. Did you write while you served?

RS: No, and I don't intend to write about my service directly. In the military there is a saying, "there is nothing more boring than an old hero."

AM: This may seem like a problematic question if not taken to refer to chronology, but were you a doctor or a soldier first?

RS: A physician must always be a physician first; anything else is unacceptable.

AM: You're the father of seven. How have you maintained your sanity?

RS: You would be surprised—it was hard at times—but it all flew by so fast. Now I only have one child left at home and it's quite sad.

AM: Do you consider yourself a Southern author? How about a Southerner?

RS: I am a Southerner. I wrote a whole essay on the perils and pressures of being a Mississippi (Southern) author. I still have some growing to do to fit into those pants, so I can only say, I hope to be.

AM: Thanks for the interview. Best of luck fitting into those pants.

Elizabeth Harris

AM: I appreciate your taking the time to do this interview. Your writing has been called "literary fiction." Your prose is beautiful and complex, allusive and fluid. The first pages of *Mayhem* call attention to "a crime whose mention makes men cross their legs," locate readers in early 20th century Texas, and reference Herodotus and Thucydides. Your prose is sophisticated and musical, poetic and meandering. Do you feel that popular fiction today lacks the lyricism and complexity that characterize so-called literary fiction? Do you feel that literary fiction is a fair characterization of your work, or perhaps that all fiction should, in essence, be literary?

EH: Thank you for your kind remarks on this semi-crime novel about a Texas woman in the early 20th century. I love good writing. And I do see much published fiction I wish had been better written—sometimes my fingers twitch for a pencil to edit a book into the better work I can see hidden in it. But lyricism seems to me a stylistic choice apart from "good writing," and I certainly wouldn't want to see everybody writing the same style. For me, part of the delight in reading is the rich variety available. For instance, besides fiction called "literary" and some detective, historical, and young adult, I read history, biography, a little theology, and the occasional targeted self-help book. *Quiet*, about being an introvert, was important to me; also David Burns's *Feeling Good*, about depression.

I suppose the term "literary fiction" is useful to readers in finding the books they want, or reviewers and booksellers wouldn't use it. Depending on how we understand it, "literary fiction" could be a fair characterization of *Mayhem*, but we don't all understand the term in the same way. I was getting questions about it last night on Writer's Chat Room. To some readers it sounds snobbish or exclusionary. Although I've read agents' websites that call literary fiction "character driven," as opposed to "plot driven," which applies only to a slice of modern and contemporary fiction—as I've incidentally suggested in a short piece about Michael Ondaatje's *The Cat's Table*.

I've heard literary fiction more convincingly characterized as focusing attention on language—and now we're getting back towards *Mayhem*. But lyricism is only one way for language to be foregrounded, which is what happens when it attempts art. Think of fiction by Mark Twain, Gertrude Stein, Ernest Hemingway (who, granted, also has a lyrical side), Raymond Chandler, James Cain, J. D Salinger (in *The Catcher in the Rye*), John Edgar Wideman, who all variously draw attention to language by means of colloquialism, rhythm, and tone.

Allen, I'm flattered and delighted that *Mayhem*'s focus on language pleases you, as I hope it does other readers. I think "literary fiction" is a fair characterization of *Mayhem* if readers can strip away the connotations of "a dull book we had to read in high school." If not, I'd replace the term with "everything else," which a friend of mine proposes—so we would have a marketing category for *Mayhem*, which is partly a fictional woman's "her-story" and partly a historically-set crime novel. My ideal (everybody needs an ideal) would be to produce books that are brilliantly written and gripping, fascinating.

AM: What is the "mayhem" referred to in your title?

EH: The mayhems I was most aware of when working on the novel were the most dramatic two, the castration of Charlie McCoy and the metaphoric cutting off of Evelyn, this traditional and deeply-rooted Central Texas woman from her family and—apart from her involvement in the incident—from her history and prior social identity. But I chose the title because it seemed resonant beyond those.

I didn't think through how: I don't do lit. crit. on my own

work except to solve problems. I've learned from reviewers to see that the gender ideas contributing to the novel's complex crime also represent a cutting of connection, as do the racial ones that condition Evelyn's delivery to her next life.

AM: How did you come to write about women in Central Texas during this time period, and how did your childhood in Texas shape this narrative?

EH: The time setting, roughly 1917-1954, was given by the decision to include certain backstories about vigilante justice and about the Civil War in Central Texas, and by the need to establish Evelyn's life as a geriatric nurse before World War Two. During and after that war, white women's employment opportunities outside small towns expanded so enormously that Evelyn would've needed complicating reasons, even at first, to stay and labor "for room and board and a few dollars a week" in this town where she is ostracized by almost everybody.

There's a lot from my Texas childhood in this novel. As you, Allen, might guess from having read it, the idea for it derived from my childhood encounters with the "live-in" geriatric nurses of some elderly relatives—some of whom could barely afford them—and from my interest, afterwards recalled periodically, in who these women were. There had always seemed to be a story about them nobody would tell me. So I wrote the novel, as the author-character claims, to imagine one of those stories—although some other things the author-character says about herself in the novel are entirely fictional. And many other bits of childhood observation and family lore contributed to the novel's design. For instance, to show me how disastrously certain men, even with good intentions, could behave towards girls and women. To set up a river with a shared fishing camp on it such as some older members of my family used to host family reunions. To create one important character, the outspoken, bed-ridden Baptist Mrs. Theriot—although the main characters, except the author, are wholly fictional. To imagine the daily labor of landowning rural folk, which I saw every time I visited an aunt and uncle of mine on the other side of the family, who were stock farmers. I could write a very long list of how my childhood helped shape the narrative, but you get the idea.

AM: What makes you write?

EH: It's fun, in that painful, demanding way that maybe running marathons—which I don't do—is fun. Writing is the thing I do that takes all of me, that absorbs me completely.

AM: Your first book was a collection of stories. What made you turn to the novel?

EH: The novel was my first love, for the way you can disappear into one, and, then, when you have to come out and leave it, you know it's still there and you can go back into it whenever you have the time. But I love all kinds of stories: telling a story is for me the most natural way to engage a situation. This is characteristic of what are apparently called "narrative thinkers': people who, if you ask them how their day was, will tell you a story. But it may also be culturally learned in Southern families. When I began to write fiction I wrote short pieces, as many writers do, because they seem more manageable, you can see the whole thing at once, and that helps when you know that you don't know what you're doing. But one of the things I discovered in writing some stories in *The Ant Generator* was that the situations that interest me most often go deep in time and character. I really am a novelist.

AM: Would you describe yourself as a reader or a writer first?

EH: Oh, a reader. As unappetizing as the idea is to me of living without writing, I was a reader before I could write, and I will be a reader after I can't write, if I live to that point.

AM: Do you write every day?

EH: Every day but Sunday, under ordinary circumstances. Sabbath time, whenever I take it, is essential to health and love and community and my writing as well as I can the rest of the time.

AM: If you could read only three books ever again, what would they be?

EH: What a horrible thought! If they had to be novels, I'd be like that character in Evelyn Waugh's *A Handful of Dust*, who ends up held captive in the jungle by a nutcase who demands that he read Dickens to him for the rest of his life. Fortunately, you said, "books," not "novels." Much as I love novels, there are no three novels I'd want to read for the rest of my life.

All the same, my mind leaps instantly to ways to cheat. Like, my big book from graduate school, *The Complete Works of Shakespeare*, which I never spent enough time with. That would give me drama and poetry. Then—still looking for ways to cheat—maybe *The Bible*, partly since there are so many different books and genres in it. And, for a third book, if I'm allowed two volumes and a magnifying glass, *The Oxford English Dictionary*, not the e-edition but the one with all the historical word derivations. There's more than enough fascination in that for the rest of my life.

AM: Religion is important in *Mayhem*. Are you a religious person?

EH: In my resolutely unorthodox way, I am, and happy in a church that welcomes people like me (so please, good folks who think yours will save my soul, bless you, but don't try). I believe in Christianity as a way, a practice. Religion is important in *Mayhem* because churches were/are socially important in small towns in the South—thus a dramatic resource for a novel set partly in one. The main religious characters are meant to practice Christian forgiveness where others make categorical gender judgments of a woman found in an ambiguous situation who is, in fictive fact, suffering from PTSD. Several of these characters are clerical, and I was recalling how—before the Civil Rights era famously revealed this—certain religious leaders might cautiously cross racial lines, transgress other social mores in witness, and get away with it because of their position. I also became interested, working on *Mayhem*, in how Christianity has interacted with the ancient honor-shame culture, which it historically softened and interiorized. (An excellent book on this is Bertram Wyatt-Brown's *Southern Honor*, which helped me write the novel.) In American Christianity there's been a more recent backlash of that ancient tribal culture, creating an ugly public "religious" culture of judgment and shaming.

And in case that's more than anybody wanted to encounter about religion here, I should add I might be a little overenthusiastic about the topic, since *Mayhem* is the first piece I've written that engages it.

AM: Thank you for taking the time to discuss your writing with us. I wish you the best with *Mayhem* and all your future projects.

Lindsay Parnell

AM: Thanks for taking the time to talk to *Southern Literary Review* about your novel, *Dogwood*. This is a remarkable and poignant book, literary fiction at its finest. You toy with stream-of-consciousness and alternating narration in the book. Why?

LP: The articulation of Harper's journey and the journey itself are irreversibility fused together. Harper's story is one of becoming, one that is bruised with digressions, but it still is rooted in the evolution of female identity and voice. Structure and content married early on in my drafting; her narrative very much showed and spoke for itself so I feel incredibly lucky. Looking back I don't think there was any other way for her story to be told. I think to present Harper's story in a more linear way, both in time frame and perspective, would be a manipulation and disservice to her act of storytelling. Harper's voice and corresponding narrative structure were birthed at the intersection of two of my favorite declarations: "it takes a story to make a story," Flannery O'Connor, and "one can confess and lie forever," Anne Sexton.

I think *Dogwood* is largely defined by Harper's often-chaotic recreation and rebuilding of ricocheting memories. Stream-of-consciousness and alternating narration both serve Harper's telling by allowing her act of telling to mirror the content of her telling. She initiates a highly considered resurrection of stories and voices chosen for her to speak in the now, and to Job. By anchoring her telling in the reconstructed memories, the reader is prompted to immediately challenge Harper's truth and authenticity as a storyteller. She struggles to articulate her history and her reality, but by her own admission, she speaks a selective truth at best. She declares herself a liar repeatedly, calling into question the "legitimacy" of her recalled incidents. Yet as a storyteller, she is plagued with lapses of self-loathing. She doesn't want to be saved. A general sense of bedlam infects her memories and in recreating these experiences, which are predominately embedded in violence, anger and confusion, the accuracy of such tellings is threatened. In turn, Harper often employs language as a defensive assault, particularly in manic episodes where narration slips from distant third to first and are unpunctuated and unbreaking and interrogating the boundaries of her speech. She's dismantling the experience itself. I hoped to bring Harper's acts of written and spoken confession to closely mirror the experience of reading the book itself, one which is often wrought with disorder and perpetual movement.

Employing stream-of-consciousness as Harper's mode of narrative also fosters the use of dialect. For me speech and voice are the cornerstones of text which I'm most drawn to and excited by. Throughout revisions the dialect has remained untouched. I didn't want anything in the text to be sanitized. I wanted the way these characters spoke and the things of which they spoke of to embody both lyrical cadence and a sense of decay. Harper's story necessitates language and speech that is cyclical and repetitive but able to refute, lie and contradict itself. Language itself alongside the rhythm and pacing of Caro and Harper and Collier's voices needed to imitate their collective physicality as well. Speech and the female body are interconnected in Harper's story; I believe the sprawling nature of stream-of-consciousness supports such a union.

AM: Your writing has been compared to that of Faulkner and Flannery O'Connor. What do you think of this comparison?

LP: I think it's exponentially generous. I desperately chase them both. The components of literature that excite, stimulate and challenge me are all anchored in their canons. For me there are no others who speak the gospel of craft and story and voice as they do, *Wise Blood* and *Light in August* particularly. I believe they write with an unmatched depth and potency of language while defying all narrative limitations. They're courageous. They write with purpose and conviction; they are titans not only of Southern artists but of American Literature.

I think O'Connor's *A Prayer Journal* has recently become one of my favorite texts on writing. It's as stirring and redemptive as her fiction. Just pages and pages of profound meditations on her process, faith as related to her artistic endeavor and frustrations, and uncertainty about her ability to write. I found this particular aspect astounding—that she would possess such doubt. I look to her and Faulkner constantly, to be inspired, to learn, to covet, to devour and to escape.

I very much hope that my fiction honors those whose work is imprinted upon me.

AM: Is it fair to say that the most important relationships in *Dogwood* are between women?

LP: Absolutely—the book's concentrated focus is cast onto the stories, voices and silence of women. Caro and Harper and Collier are bound together and at times seem to exist for each other. They share an intensely complicated history and Harper's unforeseen departure fractures their unifying relationship as a whole. They believe individually that their existence and voice are contingent on the presence and strength of the others. I think they all possess the empty notion that everything will fall into place upon the return of Harper, that somehow her presence as the crux of this trio will save them. I find that there is a great complexity to the overarching relationship of the three. They are as violent as they are deeply affectionate towards one another. Violence and what they believe to be outward expressions of love are tightly intertwined, I don't think they are able to clearly distinguish between the two. I believe that Harper assumes responsibility for the welfare of Collier and Caro both and, in turn, they both rely on her fully for protection and love. Yet, following her homecoming, Harper must discard the notion of trying to "save" their trifecta because she cannot save herself, an idea that she often transfers onto Caro, and she must accept this as one of her greatest failures. Because of this failure, Harper is haunted by the voices of her childhood and adolescence, voices that finally move her to action, to script a history, a warning which will save other girls.

The trio of Caro and Harper and Collier are the driving force of the novel but I think it was critical to include the peripheral presence of women who would challenge and shape them into being. It was very important for me to feature relationships between women who have been largely omitted from literature. They aren't debutantes or socialites. They are deeply flawed but they are women of strength and resilience. They are loyal to a fault but they are cursed, and so they curse. They assault and are assaulted. They are bruised but never broken. I wanted the varying relationships between these female characters to highlight the complexity of their identities.

I also wanted to explore the idea of inheritance through Harper, which is why it was imperative to me to present her relationship with Luce through a lens of desertion and neglect. There is a hero worship which Caro and Harper and Collier employ in regards to Luce, specifically during their childhood as they stand witness to Luce's performative femaleness. But in Harper's adulthood, Luce is a ghost of pain, violence and longing. Caro and Harper and Collier are their mothers' daughters, their greatest blessing and greatest curse.

AM: Who is Harper Haley?

LP: I believe that Harper defines herself by the events in which she has experienced, endured and ignited, but she remains uncertain to her place in the world in the absence of her mother. She's quick to call herself a prisoner, a liar, a sinner, an addict, but greatly delayed in employing an "I" in voice and in action. She's been orphaned, incarcerated, isolated and abandoned and these states are only intensified following her release from prison. Upon returning home Harper exists in a state of arrested development. She's stagnant in her "now" becoming, physically, emotionally and otherwise, and becomes enveloped in the blind loyalty to the emotional binds of her childhood, a love birth from shared history with Caro and Collier.

I never wanted to reduce Harper to a clearly definable character but the South breeds sin, storytellers and contradiction. She's deeply damaged and she's damned. She's as resilient as she is confused. She's buoyant and she's tenacious but she often succumbs to temptation. She's boundless but also still imprisoned. She is everything her mother is and is not. Harper not only creates the mythology of her mother but further solidifies it in her active participation of reverence and worship.

Harper is largely silence and, ultimately, well delayed in claiming a voice asserting an "I." As a woman she has been denied a voice, so I wanted to execute duplicity in narrative—the intentional act of claiming her own history and voice in written letters, and the emotionally distant tellings and recreations of her past. But even in speech she still adheres to a silencing: she chooses to write Job a letter in place of relaying her words on the telephone or in person. However, she's scribing a history of the women who haunt her; she's writing them into a tradition that predominantly rejects them. They speak to and through her. Harper cannot exist without the voices of Caro and Collier, Luce and Tillie, Sister Paul. Harper haunted me as much as she was haunted by the women who raised her.

One of the definitive reasons Harper even exists is because someone told me her story and voice were important. That Harper should breathe and speak the truth of her reality. Studying feminist narrative with Heidi James was beyond an education. I feel like she taught me to read as an adult. She gifted me Lynne Tillman and Kathy Acker and Angela Carter and Lydia Lunch. Heidi's own fiction is beyond instrumental in my own creative practice, and it would be a gross understatement to say that she greatly inspires my work.

AM: So you own 13 editions of *The Bell Jar* and you're happy to share a birthday with Meryl Streep. What's that about?

LP: *The Bell Jar* is one of my favorites and shortly after my first reading I wanted to own Esther Greenwood in all her published forms, so I began collecting various editions. I'm desperate for one of the few Victoria Lucas copies, as most are. I've collected a handful of *Ariel* and a couple of *Johnny Panic* but Esther and Doreen lead always.

Meryl Streep is easily one of my favorite humans. I believe she is an artist with one of the most accomplished and diverse canons across all creative mediums. Her depictions of female characters have largely shaped the voices and characters that I want to breathe life into: flawed and strong and convoluted and daring. The roles she occupies speak with conviction and passion and imagination, inhabiting heroine and villain alike, all the while conveying boundless compassion. Her roster of films is one that is built from the voices and stories of women. Also, Meryl Streep is just really fucking brilliant. I'm going to watch *Doubt* in like 15 minutes because I can't not.

AM: I agree with you about Meryl Streep. She's one of my favorites. You completed *Dogwood* in your twenties. You're still in your twenties. Not many novelists these days publish their first book before they reach 30. What was your childhood like? Were you a reader, a writer?

LP: I'm obscenely lucky to have been raised in a home where stories and the voices that tell them are not only valued but encouraged. I realized very recently that such a household can be a rarity. My parents have always emphasized the importance of words and storytelling. They're both passionate learners, so reading was something in our home that was a joyful and intimate act. It still is.

My mother and father are feminists who love words and are driven by faith. I couldn't have asked for more.

AM: There's something biblical about your novel, no?

LP: Absolutely. Many of the fictional texts I'm drawn to are very deeply rooted in Biblical narrative and language, whether it is within the continuance of tradition or an interrogation of ritual. Specifically, O'Connor, Faulkner, Dorothy Allison and Harry Crews. I've read *Bastard Out of Carolina* and *Feast of Snakes* more times than I can count because of this.

I find Biblical narrative an integral component of the fiction, poetry, visual art and music created in the South; it's woven into the fabric of Southern storytelling. I'm quite fixated on narrative interpretations of temptation, sin and guilt. O'Connor said, "drama is birthed from original sin." I couldn't be more jealous of such an expression, or know an observance of narrative more true. I think, especially with women, overarching notions of sin and guilt can be instilled very early on, and subsequently, breed a shame of the body, mind and spirit which is a dangerous assault on identity.

I think that there exists a perverse discipleship of sorts existing between Caro and Harper and Collier. But even then, they are the abject so they are rejected. Sinners because they sin and sinners because their mothers are. They are women who have fallen from grace but seek no redemption; they are proud and they are damned. I think the most explicit reference to Biblical narrative and Christian tradition is Harper's assertion that she reads the Bible but it still remains a book of men written by men. By writing her experiences to Job, she is claiming a history, writing herself into the very silence imposed onto her; she is amplifying her chosen voice.

AM: What do you do now, besides write?

LP: I've had various "professional" stints over the past couple of years. Mediocre tutor and nanny, lazy bartender and waitress, average editorial subordinate of medical textbooks and most recently, assistant at an immigration law firm. It was unexpected but is work that is shaping my current fiction and, hopefully, will continue to challenge and push me forward. The attorney I work for has become such a strong presence in my process and collaborating with her on a daily basis has allowed me to explicitly evaluate how and why I write and read the way I do. I never expected to find that type of reflection in work so far removed from fiction, ignorantly so. Working alongside her has illuminated narrative and language in a way that is redirecting my fiction and broadening my understanding of craft entirely. She has a stunning command of language and I hope very selfishly that it's contagious.

I also play a number of ukulele Amy Winehouse covers, so there's that as well. I do the Roots too, and very occasionally, Edith Piaf.

AM: I won't ask for your thoughts on the recent Amy Winehouse documentary. I take it you plan to write more novels?

LP: Shortly after *Dogwood* went to the printer I returned to short form both in reading and drafting. Angela Carter, Ann Beattie, JT Leroy and Carson McCullers, especially. Sprinting in this way I think was really beneficial in preparing for a new project. I've been drafting longhand notes for a novel for the past few years so I'm now desperate to find the courage to sit down and begin typing.

As *Dogwood* is focused on a homecoming, I'm excited to pursue an exodus. This one follows the runaway daughter of a miner, a Korean War veteran, and a Stella Adler School dropout. I can't shake off trifectas at the moment.

AM: Your book is set in the South. You were raised in Virginia. As I sit here the television is flashing with images of the Confederate flag and debates about its removal from public spaces. What does the South mean to you?

LP: I think the South is largely defined and simultaneously plagued by its contradictions, ones that tragically violate and silence members of its own population. It's an empire splintering with long set fractures, and is somehow simultaneously haunted by its past and present. I believe that to not only enable the existence of such divisions, but also to celebrate them, will not only perpetuate intolerant breaks, but also continue to silence, violently oppress and threaten lives.

Amidst turmoil, the South still thrives in tradition and in practice with storytellers and artists who are progressive, fearless, and exhilarating. Ones who challenge symbols of hatred and ones whose resilience, strength and survival prevail against adversity. *The Bluest Eye, Bastard Out of Carolina,* and *Fay* all interrogate as fiercely as they resurrect the voices of those silenced. Southern artists pulse with voices unspoken, breathing poetry into those who cannot speak themselves.

AM: Thank you for doing this interview. I hope we cross paths again in the future.

LP: Cheers, Allen!

Hubert Crouch

AM: Thanks for taking the time to talk to *Southern Literary Review* about *The Word*, your second novel. Jace Forman, the protagonist of your first novel, *Cried For No One*, is back in this novel. How has your experience as a trial lawyer shaped Jace's character, if at all? Is it even possible to identify where your legal background has shaped your character development?

HC: I leaned heavily on my experiences as a trial lawyer while creating Jace Forman. I actually know how it feels to try "high-stakes" lawsuits—the intense pressure, the sleepless nights, the perpetual gnawing in your stomach—because I have lived through them. What a trial lawyer goes through in his professional life has a profound impact on his personal life—again, I felt I was able to portray that realistically with Jace because personal experience was a good teacher. I am not saying Jace is autobiographical—he's not. That being said, my ability to create his character was, in large part, the result of having been a trial lawyer myself.

AM: I'm not out of bounds in supposing that readers of *Cried For No One* will, like me, associate Ezekiel Shaw and the Brimstone Bible Church with Fred Phelps and the Westboro Baptist Church, which is featured in the book. Is there a deliberate connection?

HC: I taught Free Speech and the First Amendment to SMU undergraduates. One of the cases we discussed in class was *Snyder v. Phelps*. There were some lively exchanges between students over whether the Supreme Court got it right when they threw out the multi-million dollar judgment awarded to the Snyders. Had the Court gone too far in protecting free speech? Had the Court allowed a zealous sect to trample upon the rights of a family to bury their loved one in peace? Our classroom debate inspired me to change the factual scenario, inject a different religious issue and pit the conflicting positions against one another in a fictitious lawsuit.

AM: What made you decide to incorporate Leah Rosen and Cal Connors into the plot? Did you envision them at the outset, or did they come later, after you had already begun writing?

HC: Cal and Leah were characters from my first novel, *Cried for No One*. Leah continues her investigation into Cal's legal misdeeds in the stand-alone sequel.

AM: As someone who has never attempted to write a thriller, I'm curious about how the intricate thriller plot falls into place. How much mapping or outlining do you do before beginning the writing process, and how often is the writing process interrupted by the need to adjust or revise?

HC: Before I wrote a word of the manuscript, I drafted a detailed, chapter-by-chapter outline, which went through a number of revisions. Once the outline was finished, I began writing the novel. Some might argue that having an outline is too confining. I get that. But for me, it is important to know where I'm ultimately going to end up before I start the journey. I find there is plenty of opportunity for creativity along the way.

AM: Texas. It's big on the map and big in your book. You've been practicing law there for some time. How far back does your connection go?

HC: A long way. I graduated from Vanderbilt in 1973 and then attended SMU Law School. After receiving my law degree from SMU, I began practicing trial law in Dallas and that's what I've been doing ever since. Although I grew up in Tennessee, I felt right at home in Texas. As the old adage goes, when you prick a Texan, he bleeds Tennessee blood.

AM: Why did you dedicate this book to your female law school classmates?

HC: One of my close friends and study partners in law school was female. She was brilliant, graduating number one in our class. And yet she received few offers from the top law firms in Dallas. There could be only one explanation—she was a woman. She, along with several other of my female classmates who had encountered a similar fate, took bold action and sued some of the major firms in Dallas. A settlement was reached which opened the door to countless female law school graduates afterwards.

AM: When did you start writing fiction?

HC: Over twenty-five years ago. I wrote a manuscript that has still not been published, although I consider pulling it out of the banker's box it's been in for years and giving it a read to see if it's salvageable. After I shelved it, I was inspired to write my first novel, *Cried for No One*, by an actual lawsuit I handled involving a macabre grave robbery. I got up early each morning and wrote before going to work. The process took me years before I had a finished manuscript.

AM: Do you know what the future holds for Jace Forman? Can readers expect to see him again?

HC: I have enjoyed creating and getting to know Jace. Based upon the reviews, readers seem to like him and, if that sentiment continues, I will likely keep him around for a while.

AM: Last question, but two parts. How much research into the First Amendment went into this book? And how interested were you in First Amendment issues before you started into this book?

HC: I have studied the First Amendment, and the cases interpreting it, extensively. As mentioned above, I actually taught a course about it to SMU undergraduates. The drafters were so brilliant and far-sighted to come up with such an important enactment. We will forever be in their debt.

AM: Thank you again.

M. Maitland DeLand

AM: **Dr. DeLand, thanks for the interview. I'm thankful for the opportunity to talk with you about your debut mystery novel, *Nashville Mercy*. How did you draw on your Southern roots and medical background to develop the plot of this book?**

MMD: My entire extended family is in the medical field. Since I was a young child, even at holiday dinner there would be medical discussions. In addition to working as a physician in my own practice I also was a medical facility owner, national accreditor, and member of state and national medical boards. Each of these hats has given me unique insight into the new onsets, extricates and diversity of medical practices, hospitals and physicians. Actually, I have Northern and Southern roots: born at the Mayo Clinic, living in Baltimore, North Carolina, Florida and Louisiana. All enriching experiences.

AM: ***Nashville Mercy* is just the first in a series, right? The Kate Katelinson Series?**

MMD: Yes, it's the first installment in the series. Right now I'm writing the sequel, *Nashville Rap*, which follows Kate as she is called to investigate the mysterious death of a well-known music producer after law enforcement abandons the case.

AM: **This isn't your first book. You've also written children's books.**

MMD: Yes, I actually have a series of children's books called *The Great Katie Kate*, which educates children and parents on serious diseases and illnesses in a lighthearted and playful manner.

It's the first educational book series of its kind. I wanted to create a non-intimidating, easy dialogue between parents and children about specific diseases and syndromes affecting their lives. Need to add the Baby Santa series. In each book, Baby Santa helps his father solve a dilemma to save Christmas.

AM: Kate Katelinson's story isn't all thriller. Tell us about the elements of romance in her life.

MMD: Kate may be a natural at cracking daunting murder mysteries, but romance is a foreign frontier for her. Like many women, she longs for a true loyal love. Her problem isn't necessarily in attracting this love, as she's an intelligent beautiful woman, but in trusting love once it arrives. It's hard for her to drop the guard and suspicion that serves her so well as a reporter and to open her heart.

In *Nashville Mercy*, Kate must decide whether the man she loves has her best interests at heart or is ultimately out to destroy her and the work she holds dear.

AM: Why the Nashville setting, besides the country music connection?

MMD: Nashville is a vibrant, beautiful city that is near to my heart. Both of my children received wonderful educations and personal growth at Vanderbilt. My children each have serious medical conditions such as Type I diabetes, epilepsy and asthma and have received the highest medical care at The Vanderbilt Medical Center. Setting the Kate Katelinson series in Nashville is a way for me to pay homage to the city's colorful culture and residents that forever engage and inspire my imaginative musings.

AM: I'm curious how you came up with Kate Katelinson. Did she spontaneously arise as a fully formed character, or did you have to develop her personality in fits and starts?

MMD: Kate's power, intelligence, and determined spirit came with the initial emergence of her character. Her more vulnerable qualities on the other hand, like her fear of failure or of hurting those she loves, arose through a more subtle process aligned with her reactions to major and minor events in the plot.

AM: How do you balance your life as a writer with your life as an oncologist?

MMD: I carve out separate spaces and times during my week for both vocations—separating them is key. I find that if I designate a specific time and space for my writing, where I can tune out my other responsibilities, juggling both life passions becomes a playful, sometimes challenging, dance—it may not be easy, but it's rewarding and fun.

AM: My wife and I have friends whose three-year-old daughter is struggling with childhood leukemia, and I'm a cancer survivor myself, so I'm fascinated by your background. Would you mind talking about that aspect of your life? How did you come to do what you do as a doctor?

MMD: My dear grandmother, who was very close to me, was diagnosed with breast cancer. I then had firsthand knowledge about the scary diagnosis, the ravage of treatments, the joy of achieving goals of therapy and most of all the helplessness and firm prayers for someone so dear. This mantra of holding each and every person's life as precious has served me well. It is an honor and privilege to help all patients. The challenge of treating children with cancer is particularly painful and difficult. Families wonder why did this happen to their innocent child. Children many times don't understand and want to be a kid like everyone else. The goal is to unite all in the effort and gentle support to the family and child while delivering the best possible care. Gaining the confidence of the young patient is paramount. I have always tried to make the experience as good as it could possibly be.

AM: I often hear people say they want to be writers but are just too busy. As someone who could have resorted to this excuse but didn't, what advice do you have for these people? You seem to have made time to cultivate your literary facility.

MMD: The bottom line is that when you love something enough, you make time for it, no matter how busy you may be. I love writing, so I make the time for it, even if that means getting up earlier or going to bed later on certain days. This discipline is a way to honor my craft, passion, and overall happiness.

AM: Thank you very much for taking the time to speak with me. I hope our readers will visit your website and check out your book. All the best with the next installment.

MMD: Thank you very much! It was such a pleasure delving into the Kate Katelinson series and the vibrancy of Nashville with you.

Howard G. Franklin

AM: It's a privilege to do this interview on the occasion of the publication of your novel, *Gideon's Children*. This book is quite a bit different from your previous book, *An Irish Experience*. You've gone from travelogue to novel. What prompted the change?

HGF: Thank you, Allen, for the opportunity to connect with readers of *Southern Literary Review* and *The Literary Lawyer*, I very much appreciate it. And to answer your question, the novel actually preceded the travelogue in terms of when each was written. In the years before *An Irish Experience* was published by Inkwater Press in 2007, I wrote four novels, none of which were published. I met my wife, Linda, during the editorial process for *An Irish Experience*, and after we married the following year she read all of them and felt strongly that *Gideon's Children* could be a special book if it was rewritten. By this she meant that when it was originally created it was contemporary, but now had a historical bent and needed to include more background about the tumultuous 1960s in which it was set.

I readily agreed, and while the final version is faithful to the original manuscript, I added considerably more of the political events and music, art, and films that made the 1960s distinctive.

AM: I presume you've drawn on your own experience working in a public defender's office in rendering this narrative. How much does this book owe to that experience?

HGF: In a word, Allen: Everything! Of my four plus years serving as a Deputy Public Defender in Los Angeles County, for three of them I was stationed in the Compton Judicial District which included Compton, Lynwood, the unincorporated area known as Willowbrook, and overflow from Watts. This was during the late 1960s, with the Civil Rights Movement in full bloom.

The five public defenders, of which I was one, who staffed our office were young, idealistic, and dedicated to providing full and proper representation to our clients as part and parcel of the greater revolution that was transpiring. The judicial establishment, used to an accommodating plea-bargain arrangement, took umbrage at our efforts, and what resulted was the full-scale courtroom war depicted in *Gideon's Children*. It is fiction, but like most historical novels, based on factual events, with characters based on the real people who participated in those events.

AM: This is a lawyer-to-lawyer question—do you feel your training and experience as a lawyer has helped or hindered your writing craft? No doubt the plot of your book would not have materialized absent some legal training, but I'm referring to style itself: the way you form sentences, choose words, adjust paragraphs.

HGF: I feel that my training and experience as a lawyer helped me as a writer in terms of organizing my novels, in particular *G.C.*, which is large and multi-layered.

However, as to my style itself, I think my style abandons the influence of my legal training. I believe that my writing style is properly characterized as lyrical, which derives from the fact that over the years I have written approximately 350 poems. By that I mean my style is fluid and highly descriptive. This leads to longer, flowing sentences that contain considerable detail, and often with adjectives and adverbs that evoke emotion. What I'm trying to do is paint as complete a picture as possible for the reader, so that he or she can not only observe what's transpiring, but can almost participate.

AM: Your novel is in many ways political, but the issues it undertakes would seem to be as urgent and important and dramatic in the true stories of actual people and events. Do you feel that there's something lost in a fictionalized account of this era and these issues? Perhaps you

feel there's something gained.

HGF: Allen, as you know, because of tragic events like Ferguson, there is a growing discussion of how to reform our criminal justice system. My fervent hope is that *G.C.* can contribute to enlarging that discussion by reaching the public at large.

Now that public is leading busy lives, filled with work, children, with their crowded schedules, and social activities with friends and the extended family. So how best to capture their attention becomes the question, and I believe that the best way to do so is to entertain them with a fascinating drama that also educates them about vitally important issues while they're being entertained. In fact, I read in the newspaper the other day of a relatively new word to describe this concept, called *edutainment*.

There are numerous excellent articles and non-fiction books dealing with the serious problems in all phases of our criminal justice system, and while they are certainly contributing to the growing discussion of how important it is for America to remedy the social injustices that exist, I felt that they are not reaching the hypothetical average man and woman. On the other hand, I reasoned, a fascinating drama, a Rocky-in-the-courtroom, knock-down-drag-out battle would appeal to them, and educate them about the serious issues our criminal justice system faces, all while these readers were being entertained.

AM: Where do you see the criminal justice system continuing to fail us or to fall short?

HGF: As designed, our criminal justice system is a work of beauty, based on the concept of due process that embodies fairness and equality. However, this system is run by human beings, and unless close and careful vigilance is maintained eternally, serious problems can and do arise.

It is no secret that despite the progress that has been achieved, America has a problem with race. And compounding that problem for citizens of all colors is the issue of poverty. As the tragic events in Ferguson illustrate, our criminal justice system needs to spawn ongoing programs designed to promote the necessary understanding that leads to solid relationships between police departments and the communities they serve, including but not limited to departments that reflect a racial balance.

Next, the overwhelming caseloads in our criminal courts must be reduced by decriminalizing minor drug crimes, and having prosecutors exercise more discretion with respect to crimes such as being intoxicated in a public place. This would reduce the burden on courts and allow more careful consideration of serious cases, free up the police to deal with major crimes, and begin to reduce the caseload for overworked Public Defenders. In addition, as Governor Cuomo asked the New York State legislature for more funding to increase the number of public defenders, so must other states in order to ensure that caseloads drop to a level that allows each public defender to offer a full and proper handling of each and every case he or she is assigned.

And last but not least, our jails and prisons are in serious need of reform. Guards must be better trained; when brutality occurs, perpetrators must be punished; educational and vocational programs must be bolstered, so that, once released, prisoners can rejoin our society as productive members. This effort to reintegrate former convicts and reduce the rate of recidivism naturally requires programs to educate employers so that having committed a crime does not automatically eliminate them from being employed.

I would add that solutions to the problems in all phases of the criminal justice system have numerous facets which I have not addressed. Instead, I have confined myself to a discussion of major issues and possible solutions that I feel are compatible for interview purposes.

AM: Does *Gideon's Children* speak to any of these current issues?

HGF: Yes, Allen, it most emphatically addresses all of the above issues, except jails and prison reform. In fact, with our individual constitutional rights being eroded by the Patriot Act, the No-Fly Rule, and unrestricted government spying at all levels, and the tragic events in Ferguson, Staten Island, Cleveland, and Los Angeles propelling a growing discussion of civil rights, the relevancy of *G.C.* was never higher.

AM: *Gideon's Children* is not a thin book. It must have taken quite a bit of time to write. Could you tell us about

that process?

HGF: In answering your earlier question, I explained that I met my wife, Linda, during the editorial process for *An Irish Experience,* and that after we were married she encouraged me to rewrite the manuscript of *G.C.*, which had been created many years earlier. Linda's suggestion very much appealed to me for two reasons. First, I believed that *G.C.* carried an important message about the value of our individual constitutional rights, social justice, and the exercise of power. And secondly, I felt that over the years I had polished my ability to write by having written three other novels, a considerable amount of poetry, and *An Irish Experience*. So, with the knowledge that *G.C.*'s setting in the 1960s now made it a historical novel, thus requiring additional background about the tumultuous era, and Linda's further suggestion that the love interest of the book's lead character needed to be fleshed out, I began the rewrite.

My first step was to research each year of the 1960s, making notes on politics, music, art, films, and sports. Then, aware of the fact that the original manuscript was quite large at 941 pages, I determined that the chapters which continued on beyond the happenings in the fictional ghetto courthouse in Solina were not essential, so I deleted them to provide room to interweave the material about the 1960s without further lengthening *G.C.* Next, I sketched a loose outline of each section of the novel, and placed various parts of my research inside it chronologically, fully aware that as I approached each chapter or group of chapters on the rewrite that I would fill in my outline.

Finally, I sat down in front of my computer and began rewriting *G.C.* by retyping it line by line and page by page, sometimes making changes to words, or cutting or enlarging descriptions of places and people, altering punctuation, and slowly but steadily integrating my research notes to provide a fuller background of the era. A large number of the corrections were accomplished directly as I typed, but when new material was added I would first write it out longhand in pencil and then make additional additions or corrections on my computer screen. This process was consistent with the manner in which I have always written, as all of my creations originally find their way out of me in longhand.

I then revise by typing what I have penciled out, now using the word processor instead of a typewriter.

My work schedule was basically seven hours a day, six days a week, with rewriting happening from eight in the morning to noon, and one to three o'clock in the early afternoon. Later, usually from ten to eleven o'clock at night, I would then read what had been written earlier, making in pencil any further changes I felt necessary, which I would then retype the following morning before moving forward to new material.

Following this schedule, with cumulative breaks totaling approximately three months for vacations, the rewrite took two and three-quarter years. When it was finally complete, Linda then read and reread the manuscript, making notes of changes and corrections she wanted, which led to us working together for another two months approximately to incorporate the vast majority, but not all, of her suggestions.

So, Allen, you're right: it did take quite a bit of time, indeed, for *G.C.* to become what it is today. And my heartfelt hope is that readers will find *G.C.* both engaging and informative about crucial issues our society faces today in the areas of civil rights and the criminal justice system.

AM: Do you still travel regularly?

HGF: Yes, I do. In the past several years, Linda and I have visited England, Scotland, Ireland, and Wales, as well as toured China, Canada, and parts of Europe with groups. In late April of this year, we are traveling to France to visit Paris and then join Linda's parents for a riverboat cruise from Paris to Normandy and back.

AM: Are you still involved in the law, or have you left that world behind?

HGF: I am no longer directly involved, in that I haven't actively practiced law for many years. However, because I have never lost my passion for pursuing social justice, I have devoted much time to following civil rights issues, including reading various appellate court decisions dealing with cases in this area.

AM: Do you think good writing can be taught?

HGF: What constitutes good writing, like all art, is highly subjective in my opinion. I think that while writing programs at all levels can help one polish his or her inherent skills, the basic core must be there and cannot be taught.

AM: One last question, and I ask this with *Gideon's Children* in mind: Are you optimistic or pessimistic about the future of this country?

HGF: That's a very tough question, Allen. By nature, I am an idealist and an optimist. And though these core qualities have been tempered by experience, I remain cautiously optimistic about the future of our country.

I arrived at this opinion by looking at our history. We began poorly by slaughtering the Native Americans and stealing their lands, and almost simultaneously importing the heinous institution of slavery. However, once founded as a nation, we created a democracy that slowly but surely, and admittedly imperfectly, overcame slavery and the corrupt oligarchies of the Gilded Age to produce the freest and most prosperous society the world has ever known.

Do we face serious problems that threaten to undermine our society? Yes, indeed, both internally and externally. At home, the issue of race continues to bedevil us despite the real progress we have made, evidenced by the desegregation of schools and the Civil Rights Acts of 1964 and 1965. As recent events in Ferguson, Staten Island, Cleveland, and Los Angeles illustrate, fifty years after the accomplishments of the Civil Rights Movement we still have much room for improvement.

Then, too, the issues of poverty, income inequality, immigration, and equality for women and the gay community must be addressed, as well as the need to bolster our educational system and our infrastructure.

And that's just at home. Externally, we are threatened by the forces who falsely use religion as a basis for terrorism, as well as the serious problems of overpopulation and protecting the Earth's environment.

In the face of all these serious problems, my cautious optimism is derived from the observation that these problems were created by human beings and, therefore, can be solved if the will to do so is summoned. Overall, admittedly, the future looks bleak. But at home, and with respect to the outside world, the picture was also bleak in the 1930s and the early 1940s in the face of the Great Depression and the barbaric Nazi war machine, and we overcame. So, in a far more complex and interrelated world, my cautious hope is that in America we will once again place emphasis on what unites us, instead of upon what divides us, and together make significant progress toward solving our internal problems, thereby setting an example that allows us to argue to our fellow nations to join us in solving issues that threaten all nations.

Foolishly idealistic, my cautious optimism? Well, even if I supplement *cautious* with the adverb *very*, I can still hear the skeptics' and cynics' loud laughter, that's for sure. But what other choice do we have, other than to summon the better angels of our nature and try to be the change we want to see in our country and our world?

AM: Thanks, Howard. Those are great closing remarks.

STEPHEN ROTH

AM: Pridemore, Missouri—the setting for your novel, *A Plot for Pridemore*. Why this place in particular?

SR: Missouri has been my home for the past 26 years, so it made sense to write about a part of the country that was very familiar to me. I also felt that basing Pridemore in Missouri would allow me to start the story with something of a clean slate. Readers have preconceptions and expectations when you write about events that happen in places like Florida, Texas or Alabama. Few people living outside of the Show-Me State have a strong opinion about Missouri. I felt that could work to my advantage in portraying Pridemore as kind of a struggling Anytown, U.S.A.

AM: *A Plot for Pridemore* is your first novel. What did you find most challenging about writing the book?

SR: I think the biggest challenge for a first-time author is the lingering fear that what you are producing is not quality work. While working on *Pridemore*, I felt that I had a compelling topic, and I enjoyed writing it, but I didn't know if it was any good until people starting reading the manuscript. It was very important to me that I selected a handful of professional writers to read my first draft, in addition to the usual collection of family and friends. When my writing colleagues reported back (some with surprised looks on their faces) that they thought my book was pretty good, I was genuinely relieved. Their feedback gave me the resolve to continue improving the manuscript and to seek a publisher.

AM: I can think of characters from history and litera-

ture who seem similar to Mayor Tolliver. I'm assuming this figure didn't spring fully formed in your mind in a single moment of creative genius. How did he come about?**

SR: I would have to say that Roe Tolliver is a composite of a few different people I have known over the years. I was a newspaper reporter for much of my 20s and 30s, and I was blessed to meet a wide range of scoundrels, blowhards, narcissists, and all-around colorful characters while covering city politics and business. I also came to know many fine, capable public servants and business leaders. However, I leaned on some of the more outlandish characters from my reporting days to create Mayor Toliver. Of course, a lot of his quirks and motivations came from my imagination as well.

Incidentally, I believe that reporting is a wonderful education on how the world operates when you are a young adult. The pay and career track aren't so great, but reporting is an excellent way to learn how to write, and what to write about. You also meet an incredible array of people. Neil Young once said that he would rather travel in the ditch than in the middle of the road because he "saw more interesting people there." The same could be said of newspaper reporting.

AM: Tell us about your decision to divide the book not only into chapters but into parts. Is there any subtle significance to that decision?

SR: Since the book covers a full year, I thought it would be helpful to the reader to break the text into the three seasons when most of the action takes place: Summer, Spring, and Summer again. I have no idea if this approach added any value to *Pridemore*. You are the first person to mention the parts of the book to me.

AM: Where did you grow up?

SR: My father was involved in textiles, so we split our time between Georgia and South Carolina when I was growing up. Most of my boyhood took place in LaGrange, Georgia, which I consider to be my hometown.

AM: I lived in West Virginia for several years and came to know several "Pridemores." It's sad and sometimes eerie but also, in a way, strangely beautiful to behold once-thriv-

ing cities and towns that are now decaying, their buildings and roads in disrepair, their downtowns now ghost towns. How does this make you feel? Is this something you're passionate about? Were you making any kind of political statement in your novel by focusing on Pridemore?

SR: I did not set out to make a political statement. However, I know Pridemore's problems are shared by many American towns as the country continues its shift from a rural to an urban society. It's a very topical issue, and you don't have to look very hard to find a feature story in *The New York Times* or *Wall Street Journal* about some spunky town in the middle of nowhere that is trying to get its act together, even though there may no longer be an economic reason for it to exist. I think those stories about people pulling together to save their towns are beautiful and inspiring. Hopefully, none of those towns go to the drastic lengths that Pridemore does to revive their fortunes.

I have always loved the intimacy of the small town. The ability to get from one place to the next in just a couple of minutes, and to run into someone you know everywhere you go, are things you take for granted until you live in a city. If the evening news is any indication, those places on the map where you can leave your front door unlocked or let your kids walk alone to a friend's house are rapidly disappearing. In Pridemore, Missouri, I tried to create a place with that small-town intimacy that readers could believe and visualize. I've been told by a handful of readers that Pridemore reminds them of the towns they knew growing up. I love hearing that.

AM: It's unusual to ask an author about his publisher, but I want to do so only because Mercer University Press seems to be coming out with several books, like yours, that readers of contemporary Southern literature will appreciate and enjoy. What caused you to submit to Mercer?

SR: A few years ago, I started sending out query letters to agents and publishers, but I had not considered pitching *A Plot for Pridemore* to a university press. Then, in 2011, I attended the Chattahoochee Valley Writers Conference in Columbus, Georgia, where I met Marc Jolley, who is director of Mercer University Press. He encouraged me to enter my manuscript in Mercer's annual contest for the Ferrol Sams Fiction Award. I submitted *Pridemore* and, a few months later, received an email from Dr. Jolley asking me to call him. Lo and behold, my book won, and part of the award was a publishing contract. I feel very fortunate to have run into Dr. Jolley in Columbus.

Mercer University Press does produce an impressive number of books, both fiction and non-fiction, that any lover of Southern culture would enjoy.

AM: Just a couple more questions. First, *A Plot for Pridemore* features an interesting relationship between Pete and Angela. What motivated this part of the book?

SR: One of my goals in the book was to give each of the main characters a dark side that would lend them more authenticity. There are no white knights arriving to save the day in *A Plot for Pridemore*. Pete Schaefer is the newspaper reporter for the *Pridemore Evening Headlight* whose job it is to unravel the mayor's devious plan to save the town. I could have drawn Pete as a bona fide good guy, but that just didn't seem right. His relationship with Angela reveals a different layer to Pete's personality that even he finds to be a little unsettling.

AM: You were born in LaGrange, Georgia, and now live in Kansas City. Do you feel that Southern authors are underappreciated at the national and even international level?

SR: Everyone has their own opinion of the South, much of it having to do with politics. I believe that many Americans have an appreciation for the rich cultural gifts the South has given us, from music to cuisine to literature. I don't think that Southern authors as a whole are underappreciated. I do think that some of the South's finest literary writers, from Ron Rash to Charles Portis to Terry Kay, have not received the public acclaim they deserve, but that's probably true of any genre of fiction.

AM: Thanks, Stephen. Here's to *Pridemore* getting the acclaim it deserves.

Paul A. Cantor

AM: Thanks for doing this interview, Paul. Your latest book is *Shakespeare's Roman Trilogy*, which analyzes three plays: *Coriolanus, Julius Caesar*, and *Antony and Cleopatra*. Could you speak to the themes of freedom and independence in the Roman Republic as against the Roman Empire?

PC: My book views the three Roman plays as a trilogy, portraying the rise and fall of the Roman Republic, and its transformation into the Roman Empire. For Shakespeare, as for many thinkers, the Roman Republic is a world of citizens, the Roman Empire a world of subjects. In the Republic, the Romans have a say in their own destiny, which concretely means that they participate in the political life of the city. In the Empire, they cede control of their lives to the Emperor, becoming the passive subjects of a remote ruler. Cassius sums it all up when he complains of Julius Caesar's incipient imperial rule: "The fault, dear Brutus, is not in our stars, / But in ourselves, that we are underlings." Here is the spirit of the Republic—Cassius will not pass the buck to some kind of fatalism, but takes responsibility for his status in the city.

AM: We're talking here for a libertarian audience. What will libertarians gain from this book?

PC: First of all, I have to say that I don't think that Shakespeare was what we think of as a libertarian. He does not display much interest in economic liberty or free markets. But he was interested in political liberty and that's what the Roman Republic represented for him.

The republican regime worked to prevent the emergence of one-man rule in the city, which the Romans regarded as tyranny. Shakespeare noted just what the American Founding Fathers did when they turned to Rome as a model for the U.S. Constitution: separation of powers and checks and balances. The overarching theme of the Roman plays is the corruption of the republican constitution as a result of foreign conquests, and the consequent emergence of Caesarism. These issues are still very much relevant to us today.

AM: How are they relevant?

PC: One thing libertarians in the U.S. today criticize is the way that the Constitution has been corrupted over the years. It was to a large extent conceived originally in a libertarian spirit, as a way of limiting the powers of the central government. But just as Shakespeare shows happening in ancient Rome, America's involvement in foreign wars led to an exponential growth in the power of the central government. In particular, it led to a massive increase in the role of the executive power in the U.S. and specifically the emergence of an imperial presidency. Based on what Shakespeare knew of Rome, he would have recognized this development easily. In Shakespeare's Rome, it takes the form of Caesarism—the great military leader assuming dictatorial control over the community. The United States has not experienced exactly this phenomenon, but a disproportionate number of its presidents based their political careers on their military exploits. That's something that should trouble us, and Shakespeare's portrait of Julius Caesar can help us think about it.

AM: If Shakespeare's interest seems to be in republican government, how should we read his rendering of militarist, imperialist foreign policy in *Julius Caesar* and *Antony and Cleopatra*?

PC: We should never forget that Shakespeare had a tragic view of life. He did not think that there is any permanent solution to human problems, and if things eventually went wrong in the Roman Republic, that's par for the tragic course for Shakespeare. He deeply admired aristocratic virtue, and for him that manifests itself largely in war. Shakespeare's tragic heroes are almost all military leaders in one form or another. I believe that Shakespeare felt that the Roman Republic had a pretty good run—nearly 450 years from the days of Coriolanus to the days of Julius Caesar. That's about twice as long as the U.S. Constitution has lasted as of this moment. So Rome's political achievement is impressive. Rome conquered the Mediterranean world and produced a remarkable series of martial heroes in the process. Eventually Rome was corrupted by its very success and its conquests subverted the republican constitution. One of the central points of my book is that for Shakespeare, the story of the Roman Republic is a tragedy. Like one of its heroes, the Republic was eventually destroyed by its own success.

AM: Does money factor into the gradual transition from polis to Empire in the Roman plays?

PC: Shakespeare shows that money was one of the principal factors in the corruption of the republican regime. The great generals like Pompey and Julius Caesar became fabulously wealthy by plundering the provinces they conquered and administered. With that money they were able essentially to buy political offices for themselves and their cronies. Moreover, they paid their soldiers directly from their war booty. Thus, their armies became directly loyal to them, and no longer to Rome. Thus, when Julius Caesar crossed the Rubicon and marched on Rome, he knew that his soldiers would stay loyal to him and ignore the Senate's orders against him. We probably don't need the lesson from Shakespeare, but he does teach that money is an incredibly corrupting force in politics.

AM: Shakespeare's Roman plays were of course written during a particular time and at a particular place. What political warnings might they have conveyed to the British monarch?

PC: I believe that Shakespeare was cautioning the Stuart monarchs against their creeping absolutism and encouraging them to remake the monarchy on the model of the Roman Republic. He hoped that without formally abolishing monarchy, the British could adopt something like the Roman mixed regime. As Shakespeare shows in *Henry V,* the ideal British king would give the nobles and the common people a sense that they have a stake in the regime and even an active role to play in it. It may sound crazy, but I believe that Shakespeare played a role in the way that the British developed a constitutional monarchy, with checks and balances on the king's power. By the eighteenth century, Montesquieu was describing Britain as a republic masquerading as a monarchy.

AM: The plebeians play interesting roles in *Coriolanus* and *Julius Caesar*, yet they're absent in *Antony and Cleopatra*. Is this absence significant? What does it mean?

PC: The turning point of Shakespeare's Roman trilogy occurs in the middle of Act III of *Julius Caesar*. The plebeians in effect decide the issue of Republic vs. Empire by siding with the imperial party of Mark Antony and Octavius Caesar against the republican party of Brutus and Cassius. They take Antony's bribe of 75 drachmas apiece to give up their active role in the regime. Even before, when they proclaim that Brutus should be Caesar, they have opted for one-man rule in Rome. Rome will have a Caesar: the only question is: which one? After the plebeians abdicate their power, they have one brief fling as rioters and then they are seen no more in Shakespeare's Roman plays. The plebeians were active in checking and balancing power in the Republic; once they become passive spectators of the action, Rome descends into imperial rule.

AM: Part of Shakespeare's brilliance involves his ability to be all things to all people—that is, to appeal to audiences with different backgrounds, perspectives, nationalities, and politics. How cautious should libertarians be about reading Shakespeare's work with an eye toward affirming their convictions?

PC: Shakespeare had an uncanny mimetic power. Because he could do such a great job of representing the world, it's easy for people to look at his plays and take whatever their favorite categories are for analyzing the world and use them to analyze Shakespeare's plays. And because of Shakespeare's prestige and genuine greatness, we all want him to share whatever our personal convictions may be. That's why Shakespeare always looks Marxist to Marxists. But as much as I wish Shakespeare were a libertarian, I have to say that I don't believe he was. He admired heroic, aristocratic virtue, not commercial, middle-class virtue. That is why you'll never see a businessman as the hero of a Shakespeare play. And I must come back to the fact that Shakespeare wrote tragedies. That's a very important fact about Shakespeare, the full consequences of which are often lost sight of. Libertarianism is emphatically not a tragic view of life. It rests on the Enlightenment idea that if we follow the middle-class virtues, we can live together in peace and prosperity. Shakespeare explores that view of life in his comedies, but his tragedies—which seem so much more fundamental to us—portray a world in which conflict is more central to human existence than harmony.

AM: In what ways was Shakespeare, in your words, "one of the most profound thinkers on the subject of ancient Rome"?

PC: Many people mistakenly believe that Shakespeare knew nothing about ancient Rome; that his Romans are merely Elizabethan Englishmen dressed up in togas. But in fact Shakespeare understood very well what distinguishes the Roman Republic as a community and what its distinctive place in history is. He understood how a republic differs from a monarchy, and he understood how a pagan community differs from a Christian one. He uses his Roman plays to explore what happens when a pagan republic focuses its activity almost exclusively on political life. Thus Shakespeare is an important figure in a long line of thinkers for whom understanding ancient Rome was central to understanding something more general about the human condition. He almost certainly knew Machiavelli's work on Rome, and as I show at length in my book, Shakespeare's view of Rome can be profitably compared with Nietzsche's. I also bring up Montesquieu in my book and even have a brief section comparing Shakespeare and Hegel on Rome. Shakespeare is worthy of being compared with such great thinkers and indeed it turns out that his understanding of Rome is very similar.

AM: You've devoted much of your career to Shakespeare. When did you first become interested in him?

PC: I grew up in a home in which literature was taken very seriously. My grandfather had a Ph.D. in English and my mother had an M.A. My father was a book collector and so I grew up surrounded by books, including many editions of Shakespeare.

My older brother shared with me what he learned in literature courses at Cornell. I cannot remember exactly when I first encountered Shakespeare, but it was very early. When other kids in Brooklyn were going to Dodgers games at Ebbets Field, my mother was taking me to Stratford, Connecticut, which at that time had a very active Shakespeare Festival every summer. Perhaps the greatest theatrical experience of my life was seeing Morris Carnovsky play King Lear there. So very early on I learned the power of Shakespeare onstage. As for the academic study of Shakespeare, my 9th grade class at Meyer Levin Junior High School did a major project on *Julius Caesar,* and that's when I first learned to work on a play in depth. My interest in the Roman plays goes way back.

AM: When did you first become interested in Austrian economics? How has it shaped your career as a literary critic?

PC: I first became interested in Austrian economics when I was 13 or 14 years old. My brother Donald was then at NYU law school and studying with the great labor law professor, Sylvester Petro, who was a friend of Ludwig von Mises and recommended his books in his classes. Not one to mess around, I read *Human Action.* I got hooked quickly on Austrian economics and was the first kid on my block to learn the word "epistemological." When I was 15, a friend and I had the audacity to call up Mises at home and he graciously invited us to attend his NYU seminar. So I got a very good grounding in Austrian economics before I even went to college. I have not devoted my whole career to studying literature in light of Austrian economics; I have been influenced by a wide range of interpretive approaches. But starting in the 1990s with my essay on Thomas Mann and the German hyperinflation, I found many areas in which my grounding in Austrian economics helped me to understand literary works. More generally, my Austrian background led me to drop my cultural elitism and learn to appreciate the importance and greatness of commercial culture. That led to my studies of movies and television—perhaps the best-known aspect of my career.

AM: Thank you for doing this interview, Paul. Your work at drawing libertarians to the arts and humanities is unparalleled. I hope many others follow in your footsteps.

Tom Turner

AM: Hi, Tom. Thanks for talking to us about your new novel, *Palm Beach Nasty*. **It's a crime thriller, and we don't have a chance to feature many crime thrillers—a genre that's very popular. What brought you to the genre?**

TT: Thanks for interviewing me, Allen. In answer to your question: Honestly, when I started writing—twenty years ago—I felt that I wasn't good enough to write a story without action—a murder here, a shoot-out there, maybe throw in a car chase. You know, to keep the reader engaged, turning pages. Turns out, I didn't really need that stuff, but now I like the crime novel genre so much I'd never write anything else.

AM: You used to call Palm Beach home. It's central to this story in which characters are shaped by place. There's something "Palm Beach" about them. Is there something "Palm Beach" about you? Or do you seem to adapt to your climate? You now live in Charleston, South Carolina—one of my favorite cities—and have completed a book set in Charleston.

TT: I love Palm Beach and have spent a fair amount of time there. It's got everything. Glamour, glitz, pretension, phonies, scammers, wannabes, never-will-be's and some of the greatest, down-to-earth, nicest people you'll ever meet. It is an incredible mine of material. I think it's good for ten more sequels to *Palm Beach Nasty*! Charleston, too, is a great source of material. Way different, but like Palm Beach, it's got everything.

AM: Tell us about Charlie Crawford and Mort Ortt, a pair

of cops who get set on the trail of a killer. Is it true you came up with them while working the Florida real estate market?

TT: They were amalgams of people that I know. I wanted opposites, but ones who also had a lot in common. Mort is maybe my favorite character of all. This short, squat, wheezing, profane guy who turns out can run faster and jump higher than his handsome, in-shape partner, Charlie Crawford.

AM: Why are Charlie and Mort so different?

TT: As I said in response to your previous question, imagine a short—what's a nice word for fat?—rotund guy, balding, fifty but looks like sixty, then imagine a tall, handsome Adonis.

The short guy, Ott, is easy to underestimate, that's what makes him so critical to their partnership. Plus he has insights that Crawford never has.

AM: Have you always been a writer?

TT: I started out as a copywriter in New York. And, as I'm sure you know, all copywriters think they have the great American novel in them. Maybe one did. F. Scott Fitzgerald was originally a copywriter, as were Joseph Heller, Salman Rushie, Dom DeLillo and Dorothy Sayers. I wasn't a very good copywriter and got into real estate when I was thirty. Ten years later, I started writing on the side and twenty years after that came *Palm Beach Nasty*.

AM: Do you read crime thrillers written by others? Who are your favorite authors?

TT: Yes, I do. My top two are Elmore Leonard and James Lee Burke. I could rhapsodize forever on their merits, but suffice it to say, nobody wrote dialogue and was more real than Leonard. And nobody wrote descriptions and has more vivid, impossible-to-forget characters than James Lee Burke. I also really like Lee Child, who named one of his recurring characters, Major Susan Turner, after my ex-wife, but that's another story!

AM: You worked at a private investigating firm in Florida. What was that like?

TT: I was mainly a guy who did cheating spouse investigations. Suffice it to say, it wasn't pretty and I only lasted ten months at it. Most of the experiences I have from it are X-rated and won't find their way into my novels.

AM: Did that experience influence *Palm Beach Nasty* at all?

TT: Not so much. What really influenced *Palm Beach Nasty* was my time in Palm Beach renovating and building spec houses. I dealt with a million people—contractors, buyers, sellers, real-state brokers, you-name-it—and a lot of them had some pretty interesting stories. I just gave their stories a good jolt of steroids.

AM: Your book came out in January, right? Are you going on a book tour?

TT: Yes, the book came out on January 31st. My incredible publicists—it's okay to slip a plug in here, right?—Caitlin Hamilton and Rick Summie, have me doing quite a few author talks and signings in both Charleston and the Palm Beach area. I have absolutely no clue how to do these things, so I'll just stumble and bumble my way through them. Actually, I'm really looking forward to them.

AM: Thanks for doing this interview, Tom. Best of luck at these book talks and signings, and of course with the book sales as well.

Thank you, Allen. I really appreciate the opportunity you've given me. Next time you're in Charleston, give me a call. I know where the best gin mills are!

F. Diane Pickett

AM: Hi, Diane. You were born in Atlanta. So was I, in Piedmont Hospital. And you live in Destin now, where I spent many weeks of my childhood. We've probably crossed paths at some point. Where do you do your writing down there at the beach?

FDP: I was born at Emory University Hospital. I do my writing at my little cottage in Sandestin which I have named Magnolia Manor. That may give you an idea of just how Southern I really am.

AM: I have here in my hands your novel, *Never Isn't Long Enough*. You state in the "Author's Note" at the beginning of the book that you "set about recreating the lives of two Southerners and their individual journeys in an attempt to reveal who they started out to be and who they actually became." Could you elaborate on this?

FDP: The two main characters are a young farm girl and a wealthy, sophisticated older man. The young girl left the farm behind and all of its remnants. The older man morphed from a carefree single life into a model of responsibility. Neither started out on either path.

AM: I find it fascinating that you thought writing the book was easier than publishing it. How could that be?

FDP: The writing came naturally, but the publishing was a *huge* and continuing learning curve of frustration. *Never* is my first novel and I have everything to learn about the book business. Hopefully, I *have* learned something as I am now working on a collection of short stories titled "Never Tell a Tall

Tale (Keep 'em short)" to be published later in the year.

AM: When did you first decide to write *Never Isn't Long Enough*? Where were you when you wrote the first sentence?

FDP: I wrote the book while I was recovering from some surgery and was at my cottage in Sandestin. There I was bored to tears with endless time on my hands, thinking about my father. I recalled something he said to me when I was a little girl. So, I just got out of bed and went to the computer and wrote that down. That prompted me to continue and next thing I knew, I had written a book.

I hadn't intended to write a book and had no idea at the time that was what I was doing.

AM: Explain your decision to reference scholarship in the book. For instance, there's a reference to Eugene Genovese and Phillip Shaw Paludan.

FDP: Since I am a novice at writing and certainly no historian, I thought it pertinent to interject some learned words that would give credence to my statements and observations. I have no writing experience and have never had a creative writing class of any sort. I was just winging it.

AM: You also incorporate actual documents, like a 1900 excerpt from the *Atlanta Journal*.

FDP: That was a true story about my grandfather and a family archive.

AM: What's your writing process? Did you have a routine, a regiment?

FDP: I have never written anything on a regular basis except thank you notes. Having been married twice, I *did* have some experience there. However, I just write when the mood strikes me. Sometimes it actually hits me in the face and other times it goes right over my head. I don't really have a routine. But, when I am in the mood, I am very disciplined and try to finish a train of thought—which usually means a chapter.

AM: Were there any authors you were trying to mimic when you wrote the novel?

FDP: I am not experienced or vain enough to try to mimic anyone, but it's a good idea. Any suggestions?

AM: You're doing just fine on your own. There's a lot of history in your novel. How much research did you have to do?

FDP: Well, at my age I have already *lived* a lot of history, so some of it was just recall. It was also helpful that my own father was born in 1900, so I had stories from him that were recalled. It was also useful that my own grandfather actually fought in the Civil War. However, I did do a lot of fact checking on dates and such.

AM: Thanks for your time and for sharing these great insights.

Colleen D. Scott

AM: Thanks for doing this interview, Colleen. Your first novel is *Everybody Needs a Bridge*, which you describe as a "work of fiction inspired by actual events." It follows the story of Erin, a young girl in Alabama who's growing up roughly a generation after the Civil Rights Movement. You might call it a bildungsroman involving friendship, race, and the burdens of history. Of course, Alabama is your home too. Were the actual events that inspired the narrative witnessed or experienced by you, or purely drawn from secondhand knowledge and basic immersion in the culture and region?

CS: It is my pleasure, Allen. Yes, the novel is intended to be a bildungsroman. The story line is a progression of events that challenge the conscience and beliefs of the main character, the majority I either experienced or witnessed firsthand. But the story line was also intended to be broader than just one person's story and represent a generation, coming of age in the south, post-civil rights. Hopefully, by reliving the experience through the eyes of the main character, the reader will be inspired to rise to similar challenges presented in society even today.

AM: What are some of those challenges?

CS: One challenge is the pressure of societal expectations which shape what we consider to be ideal. Our chosen courses of study, hobbies, occupations, our friends and even our mates are either in concert or in conflict with those expectations. It is my hope that the novel demonstrates the amazing value of relationships. With each word and action, in every relationship we form, we possess the power to either encourage or discourage those around us.

Another overarching challenge explored is the impact of social segregation. When we isolate ourselves we feel uncomfortable around others from different backgrounds, ethnicities, classes and races. I hope the novel highlights the importance of forming relationships with those different from ourselves. I fear that lately we are showing the signs that we might forget how important it is to recognize our similarities and cherish our differences.

AM: You worked in the corporate world for many years before becoming an author.

CS: Yes, primarily in finance. I had an opportunity to make a change, and since I have always enjoyed writing and am an avid reader, I decided to seize the opportunity. I have loved every minute of it and now my second novel is in the final stages of editing!

AM: *Everybody Needs a Bridge* captures those awkward teenage years in high school and all that comes with them: the laughing, the teasing, the fitting in, and worse. How did you transport yourself back to that stage of life to construct a first-person narrative?

CS: Before I began writing, I shared my personal experiences with a few close friends and found that those feelings of awkwardness, loneliness and frustration of trying to fit in were unfortunately common. The discussions helped me sharpen my memories of those emotions and they haunted me until I could leave them with the characters in the scenes of the novel.

AM: When you first sat down to write Erin's story, did you know where you were headed? Did you already have a plot in mind?

CS: Somewhat. I had the high level plot and overarching theme both in mind before I began writing. But instead of writing a detailed outline, I instead utilized poster boards as story boards and post it notes to represent the scenes and the characters. This visualization allowed me to add, delete and change scenes and characters as I wrote and the story line evolved.

AM: Did you write from home? Did you return to Alabama for inspiration or information?

CS: I primarily write either from an arm chair on my porch or a booth at a local coffee shop. Both locations allow me to get lost in my writing and block out distractions. I do return to Alabama occasionally to visit friends and relatives. When I need inspiration, I spend time at the beach. For me there is nothing more empowering than walking on the beach as the sun rises and again as it sets.

AM: Issues of race and racial identity are central to *Everybody Needs A Bridge*.

CS: Absolutely. Without understanding the dynamics of race and the impact of racism on the central characters, the reader would lose important context. But I also wanted to illustrate how through ordinary conversations and interactions we inadvertently sustain those racist attitudes. And how those small actions can be just as effective as overt and violent acts.

AM: As Erin ages, her concerns become increasingly grave and weighty. Teenage pregnancy. Murder. She enters college. She has to come to terms with life and death. I don't want to give too much away by saying anything more specific. What does it mean to become an adult? What does it mean to put away childish things?

CS: Life events have a way of forcing us into adulthood, don't they? For Erin the hallmark of entering adulthood is when she realizes the importance of accepting the consequences of her decisions. Thankfully, the crucial friendships she formed along the way clearly illustrated how adults must make decisions, move forward, and do so without assigning blame or hanging on to lingering regrets.

AM: Thank you for this interview. I look forward to reading your next novel.

David Joy

AM: We're thrilled to interview you at *Southern Literary Review*, David. Thank you. Your novel is *Where All Light Tends to Go*, a story about the underbelly of North Carolina, where outlawing is, the opening lines tell us, "as much a matter of blood as hair color and height." Tell us how Jacob McNeely, your narrator, came to be.

DJ: I saw Jacob before I heard him. And what I mean is that there was an image before there was a voice. I was at a buddy's house up in Cashiers and we were standing by his hog pen where he keeps these feral hogs he traps and he was telling me about how, when they're hunting, they kill some of the hogs with a knife. They bay the hogs with hounds and when the dogs get the pig down the hunter will go in and stab the hog in the heart. So while he was telling me this, an image came into my head, an image of a really young boy doing this. I saw a boy with his father standing behind him telling his son what to do, and this boy watching the light go out of this animal's eyes and suddenly realizing just how much power a person had over life and death.

That image stuck with me for a long time, and I kept trying to write his story, but I kept getting it wrong. I think I kept trying to force it rather than let him tell me what he wanted to tell me. Then one night I woke out of a dream and Jacob was talking. That's when I finally got it right is when I stopped trying to force it. I seemed to get it right when I started listening.

AM: You and I are about the same age. We were both born in 1983 at any rate. You must write about the places you know,

as the North Carolina setting tracks your own paths through that state. How did the region shape and influence your fiction?

DJ: North Carolina is the place and the people I know. Until this past year, I'd never really gone anywhere outside of the state. You can trace my family back in every direction and pretty much as soon as my ancestors got off the boats in Virginia they headed to the piedmont of North Carolina. This goes back to the 1700s. They were poor cotton farmers and tobacco farmers mostly. I'm very much rooted to this state and this place. But about twelve or thirteen years ago, I wound up moving to the mountains and I think a lot of that had to do with finding a very familiar value set that still existed in Appalachia, but that was quickly disappearing where I grew up. The people in the mountains remind me of my grandmother who grew up on a cotton farm and who had this very deep-seated vein of storytelling and people and culture running through her. Us Southerners are lucky in that sense, in that we come out of a very rich storytelling tradition. The writers I'm most influenced by, writers like Larry Brown and William Gay and Ron Rash and George Singleton and Harry Crews and going back to folks like O'Connor and Faulkner, all of these people are coming out of a Southern storytelling tradition. All of these writers are focused on the lives of working class people doing the best they can. Those are the footsteps I'm following, and I think that's how this region and this place shape my work.

AM: There's an element of class in the book that interests me. Jacob refers to himself as "trash" in the eyes of his peers. His dad deals "crank" and is covered in tattoos—not exactly markers of the upper echelon. His dad's girlfriend has rotting teeth. His dad and his mom talk in slang, with accents, and cuss like sailors. By contrast—and maybe this is just because it's graduation—when we first meet Maggie Jennings she seems the debutante type: wearing high heels and a white sundress, standing with the ostensibly "perfect American family" that, in fact, is living a lie, according to the narrator. What's going on with class in the novel?

DJ: The class issues that are most interesting to me in the novel are taking place in the background. Cashiers, where the story is set, is kind of a strange place as far as socio-economics, and this is something we see in the periphery, though I don't know that it ever comes fully into focus. One place in the novel that comes to mind for me is when Jacob is pulled over by the deputy and he's looking out at the lake and seeing the cigarette boats and he sees the cars loaded with out-of-towners summering in the mountains. Another example is the barge Jacob's father steals, a barge used to take "summer folks to and from their houses on Buck Knob Island in the middle of Lake Glenville. Rich folks could afford those luxuries. They could afford to build their houses in a place that no one without a fortune could get to, so they did."

Cashiers has some of the highest-end country clubs and gated communities in America. When I was writing this book, I was working two jobs and the second job was at a recreation center where Andy Roddick would come in and play basketball. That's the type of wealth that is in Cashiers in the summer. But at the same time, you've got families who go back to the first land grants. You've got names like McNeely and McCall and Dillard and Fowler and Farmer and Dills and Aiken and Rice that go back generations. These are salt-of-the-earth, working-class people. The type of stratification I'm talking about is honestly mindboggling. You've got ten million dollar homes with copper roofs right across the holler from people who are stripping the wire out of houses just to make ends meet.

You've got people who drive hundred thousand dollar cars to a grocery store where the folks working can barely afford what they're stocking on the shelves. You've got hunting dogs running bear across the fairways of Tom Fazio-designed golf courses. That's where this novel is set. And those are the class issues at play.

AM: Let's talk about drugs. They're an important part of the book. Readers might have a discussion about the political, cultural, economic, and social effects of drugs in Jacob's life.

DJ: Where I grew up and for the types of people I write about and am interested in, I think drugs represent two things. On one hand they're a source of money, an economic means for getting things that you otherwise wouldn't be able to have. But at the same time, they're also self-medication and a way to escape, albeit briefly.

We see both sides of that in the novel. We see Jacob growing up in a household where his father sells methamphetamine, and where Jacob is being groomed to do the same. And at the same time, we see Jacob's mother is an addict, Jacob is abusing prescription drugs, and his father's taking painkillers and drinking. I think I write about these things because it's what I grew up around. It's real to me. I'm certain it comes off as extreme to some, but it's been the reality of most of the people I grew up with. These are very real problems and when you're writing about lower working class lives it's unavoidable. I'm not interested in lives where everything pans out. I'm interested in lives where everything falls apart. I'm interested in how people try to navigate a world where the odds are stacked against them. The ugly truth of that reality is that oftentimes the world is just too heavy a place to bear.

AM: The plot involves the murder of Robbie Douglas. You do a fine job of walking the lines of genre. This is both a popular thriller and a work of literary fiction. Were you mindful of this tightrope walk as you pieced the book together?

DJ: I was definitely conscious of how I wanted the narrative to move, and I think that's why it meant so much that Daniel Woodrell said the novel had "a graceful but restless pace." He's one of my idols and in a lot of ways he was the writer I was trying to emulate. A novel like *Tomato Red*, you read the opening line and you're at the end of the first chapter before you come up for air. I remember the first time I read that novel, I spent an entire day reading the opening chapter over and over trying to figure out how he did it, how he was able to hold me in the palm of his hand. Daniel's definitely a master of that, especially with that stretch from *Tomato Red*, *Death of Sweet Mister*, and *Winter's Bone*. Barry Hannah's another that comes to mind. Larry Brown does this with *Father and Son*. Donald Ray Pollock is another. Even someone like Ron Rash, who I think is writing some of the most poetic fiction in America, you can look at the stories in a collection like *Burning Bright* and you can see how he's in full control of how fast the narrative is moving. All the writers I really admire are very aware of that pedal. They know when to hit the gas.

AM: Your second novel is forthcoming. You're probably still wrapping it up. Before I ask about it, I'd like to know

a bit about your writing habits: your schedule, where you write, how often—that kind of thing.

DJ: Just finished the new novel, and my process still seems to be evolving in a lot of ways. For years, I thought to be a writer you had to sit down and write every day. That's something I've never been able to do, so for a long time I felt inadequate, like I was doing something wrong. Then one day I ran across this interview with Raymond Carver in the *Paris Review* where he's talking about his process and what he said described how I work to a tee. Carver said, "When I'm writing, I write every day. It's lovely when that's happening. One day dovetailing into the next. Sometimes I don't even know what day of the week it is. The 'paddle-wheel of days,' John Ashbery has called it. When I'm not writing…it's as if I've never written a word or had any desire to write. I fall into bad habits. I stay up too late and sleep in too long. But it's okay. I've learned to be patient and to bide my time. I had to learn that a long time ago. Patience."

I think that idea of fits and starts, and that idea of long spells where I feel like I've never written anything in my life and then all of it suddenly surging out at once is something that is very much definitive of my process. And just like Carver said, I'm trying to get to a place where I'm patient and trust in knowing that the story will come. Silas House said one time that he writes 24/7, and what he meant by that was that even when he's not putting words on the page, he's thinking about things. He's thinking about characters, picking up little pieces from the world around him, and all of that eventually makes it into the story. So for me, it's important to remember that the times when I'm not writing are just as essential, maybe even more so. My process is also evolving in a lot of ways because of deadlines, and I find that I work much better at night. When I'm really cooking with gas seems to be from about midnight to somewhere around five in the morning. When the writing is coming like that I keep really strange hours. Usually I'll get up around nine in the morning and work till lunch, eat lunch and then nap for an hour or two. Then I'll work till supper and take another nap. After that I'll work all night until about five. I'm usually sleeping seven or eight hours a day, but it's broken up into all these small segments of time. You might find me pacing the front yard or walking down the road at four in the morning. Makes it hard to have friends, I guess, but I'm kind of an odd duck anyways.

AM: And the novel you're working on now—it's tentatively titled *Waiting On the End of the World*. What's it about? Do we return to North Carolina?

DJ: Right now, I can't imagine writing anything set outside of North Carolina. That's just the landscape and people that I know. Like I said earlier, until this past year, I'd never really been outside of the state. But to answer your question, yes. The new novel is set in North Carolina, and once again it's set very specifically in Jackson County where I live, this time in a community called Little Canada. I have a hard time answering what a book's *about*. That always seems like a philosophical question and to steal a line from Donald Ray Pollock, "I'm probably the least cerebral guy you're ever going to meet as a writer." But I think the big picture is that this new book is about trauma and how different people cope with trauma, how the things we witness, the things we carry, come to govern our lives. As far as what happens in the book, or the trigger for the narrative, there are these two best friends, Aiden McCall and Thad Broom, who go to buy drugs and wind up witnessing the accidental suicide of their dealer. All of a sudden a riot of meth and money lands in their laps and what ensues is a meth-fueled race toward disaster. That's the set up.

AM: Thanks for this interview, David. What's the best way for readers to follow you and keep up with the novel and your goings-on?

DJ: At the advice of folks who know much more about such things than me, I've got accounts on Facebook and Twitter and Instagram and you can get to those from my website. My website is also a good place to see where I'll be for readings and events. I love meeting people and talking books and hearing stories so that'll always be the best way: just come hang out at an event at a local bookstore or somewhere. Plus, if it's a real honest-to-god, face-to-face conversation, we can drink beer afterward and that beats the hell out of computers.

AM: Again, thank you. All the best.

DJ: Thank you.

Mark Schimmoeller

AM: Mark, I'm excited about this interview because I'd like to say I know someone who made a cross-country trip on a unicycle. Not many people can claim that—probably just the people who know you. Why in the world did you undertake this journey?

MS: I'm thrilled that you know a cross-country unicycle traveler—and a bit envious, for I've yet to meet one (or even hear about one) since I took my journey in 1992. I suspect our numbers are on the low side, though sometimes I entertain myself by seeing them often, in someone, say, picking up a violin for the first time, or an elderly person experimenting with a walker, in people who apparently aren't getting anywhere but who are nonetheless absorbed in a task. Why did I take off on a unicycle? Because I wanted to give myself all the time in the world. As I say in the book, I wanted to squander time (as most people would view unicycling) in order to demonstrate its availability.

AM: Your book about this journey is *Slowspoke*, with the subtitle *A Unicyclist's Guide to America*. For those who haven't read the book, what do you mean by "slowspoke"?

MS: With this title I'm simply trying to be descriptive of a spoke on a unicycle wheel, which is never spun around so quickly that it ceases to move. There are a lot of moving parts in the riding of a unicycle, and a unicyclist, consciously or unconsciously, is aware of them all. As a consequence of technological advances over the last couple of centuries, we as humans have become less aware of the velocities of things that support us. My journey was in some ways a response to this. I didn't want my vehicle to be incomprehensible. I wanted to see its spokes and to feel my connection to the planet.

AM: Janisse Ray says in the Foreword that your narrative "offers a love-filled and hard-hitting philosophy that asks us to search our souls for more thoughtful, conscientious, and sustainable ways of living." I'm not asking you to forfeit your humility, but what do you think she meant by this?

MS: Janisse is very kind, but my intent is not an activist one with respect to the reader—it is merely to communicate an impulse that I had to playfully slow. That impulse led me often to feel vulnerable and dismissed by our society, but also open to my environs, swayed by them and happy. If I've communicated that complexity to unicycle travel (which would be true of any endeavor that doesn't compute but that engages our minds, spirits, and bodies), then I would be delighted.

AM: Back when I was a freshman in college, my entire incoming class was assigned to read Ray's memoir *Ecology of a Cracker Childhood*. She's a talented writer. Having her praise must mean a lot. Tell me, what writers have most influenced you? While I'm at it, did you ever think of yourself as a Jack Kerouac from a later generation—perhaps a more creative or at least more athletic version of him? Your epigraph quotes Howard Zinn, and I can see that connection too.

MS: Yes, I am thrilled. *Ecology of a Cracker Childhood* is a lovely, poignant memoir. As for Kerouac, I think he has always been nearby as I've worked on *Slowspoke*. I've also been influenced by *Blue Highways* and *Zen and the Art of Motorcycle Maintenance* and even, for a comic look at progress, *A Hitchhiker's Guide to the Galaxy*. Other writers who have had a big effect on me are William Morris, Rachel Carson, Wendell Berry, Annie Dillard, Henry David Thoreau, and Edward Abbey.

I'm also an avid reader of contemporary literary novels—I'm drawn to sentences that hold as much mystery as definition, that ask me to be both reader and creator as the story unfolds.

AM: I hope you won't mind a compliment: your prose is stunning. It really is. I've tried to find the perfect passage to ask you about, but there are just too many to choose from. It's not just the stories that are poignant, but the way you're alert to things like motion, sound, place, space. Do you think you're more attentive to these things in your everyday life than other people are in their own lives? I have in mind a talk Truman Capote once gave at Auburn University. He said he believes writers are more observant and sensitive to the details around them.

MS: Thank you. If there's good prose in *Slowspoke*, it is the result of working on this book for twenty years. The sentences got better, at least most of them. This is something I choose to believe. I love revision, but it was also a good feeling to read my final draft in 2014 (the book took its form over the course of four drafts, the first two written on a manual typewriter) and to realize that it really was the final draft. Sometimes I wonder how the writing process would have been different if I had traveled across the country on a bicycle, or, heaven forbid, something motorized.

AM: You write this in the book, speaking about your unicycle hanging among the tools in your shed: "I'm occasionally disoriented by its lack of motion, and when people ask me if I'm ever going to travel on it again, I don't have a good answer." If I were to ask you that very question today, would you have a good answer?

MS: I think I would say that there's a time and a place for a journey and that it's probably better to start new ones than retake the old. Currently I'm working on a novel, living with my wife Jennifer in the woods, in an off-the-grid cabin we built with our own hands. I'm pretty much not going anywhere, which reminds me, actually, of unicycling. And, really, noticing the seasons pass by—the field on its way to a woods, our apple trees acquiring the thick trunks and limbs that you see in established orchards—gives us, at this point, the journey we're most interested in.

AM: Thank you very much for your time. If you're ever wheeling your way down to Alabama, make sure to look me up.

Richelle Putnam

AM: Thank you for talking to us about your latest book, *The Inspiring Life of Eudora Welty*. If my memory is correct, this is the first interview that *Southern Literary Review* has done about a work in the young-adult (or, as they say, YA) category. I'd like to start by asking about your decision to write this book for that audience. Was the book commissioned? Did you feel strongly about telling Welty's story to a young audience? Do you just enjoy writing in that genre? Or was it something else? Welty published her first work at age 10, so it would make sense for you to want to inspire some of the young potential Weltys out there.

RP: Thank you for interviewing me.

The History Press had just started a children's nonfiction category and they approached me about writing a biography in this category. Much of my creative writing background specifically targeted children's literature. Almost immediately I knew I wanted to write about Eudora Welty, focusing on her family heritage and the eras she and her family lived through in Jackson, Mississippi, which included Women's Suffrage, the Roaring Twenties, the Depression, two World Wars, and the Jim Crow South.

Indeed it was the determination in Eudora's early years to pursue writing that inspired me to write her story for adolescents and young adults. Her desire, determination, and perseverance in early eras that rarely supported independent, ambitious women should be an inspiration to anyone.

AM: Why Eudora Welty? What does she mean to you?

When did you first read her and what impression did she make on you that you would choose to write a book about her?

RP: Around 2005 I began researching Eudora Welty for a Mississippi Writers Guild program that honored Mississippi writers. From this research, I wrote a monologue and portrayed Eudora Welty at various locations and events around the state, including the Eudora Welty Library in Jackson and the Southern Cultural Heritage Foundation in Vicksburg. In 2009, four writer friends and I wrote a one-act play "Was It Worth It?" The characters were William Faulkner, Tennessee Williams, Richard Wright, Muna Lee and Eudora Welty. Each of us wrote the dialogue for the writer we had researched. I wrote Eudora's dialogue.

All the content in the play was historically accurate. Much of Eudora's conversation in the play was her actual words from various interviews or her memoir, *One Writer's Beginnings*. This play won 1st place in the Tallahatchie Riverfest Playwriting Competition and was showcased during the Tallahatchie Riverfest. From there, we performed the play for special events in Mississippi and in Alabama, including the Alabama Writers Conclave Writers Conference.

Each time I portrayed Eudora, I felt closer to her. She inspired me in my writing and in the pursuit to be a successful writer. I loved her spunk, admired her humility and respected her devotion to family and to her home state. Even though I never met her personally, she became my mentor in both life and writing.

AM: Although your book is about Welty, it's also about the cultural milieu in which she was born and raised. You talk a lot about Mississippi and about race relations and a bit about politics. How do you think this culture shaped Welty's fiction?

RP: Until I learned about Eudora the individual, I did not fully understand Eudora the writer. Her stories speak loudly and clearly of the times and the cultural mindset of the South. She developed her characters so honestly and blatantly, readers could view the South from the characters' perspectives. She was criticized for not "speaking out" in the 60s during the Civil Rights Movement, but if the accusers had read her work critically ("Powerhouse," "A Worn Path," "Keela," and "Where is the Voice

Coming From?" to name a few), they would have seen that she had long written about civil rights. In her essay "Must a Novelist Crusade," Eudora said: "A plot is a thousand times more unsettling than an argument which may be answered." I believe Eudora Welty was incredibly disciplined in her life and her work. That discipline was formed because of her culture and upbringing.

AM: Welty was, of course, a master of the short story, a genre that some believe is dying out—a claim I understand but don't buy into. At least not yet. Do you feel that the short story has reached its zenith and entered into its decline? Are there any Eudora Weltys out there today?

RP: To the contrary, I believe that the short story will not only survive, but flourish in the coming times. We live in a fast-paced society that is growing faster all the time. We go for fast food and quick fixes and have traded long phone conversations for short text messages. Many readers like books with short chapters they can easily stop on without feeling they left in the middle of something.

That said, short stories, whatever the genre, satisfy readers quickly. I love a good novel, memoir and history book, but I always have a collection of short stories on my bedside table and in my suitcase. Some of the greatest, most memorable literature, in my opinion, has been short stories like "The Garden Party" (Katherine Mansfield), "Everyday Use" (Alice Walker), "The Lagoon" (Joseph Conrad), and "A Rose for Emily" (William Faulkner). The power of the short story cannot be denied.

AM: You love Mississippi, don't you?

RP: I do love Mississippi, its beauty, its hospitality, its charity and its ability to produce some of the world's most renowned artists. I do believe Mississippi is misunderstood and that many who criticize Mississippi either haven't ever been here or have never been here long enough to experience the people who happily cross racial, social and cultural lines to build long-lasting friendships and relationships.

However, I never use these good traits to excuse bad behavior and negligent attitudes. The Jim Crow South damaged our country in many ways as much as the Civil War. In my opinion, we must finally recognize ourselves as a country and not as either North and South, Yankee or Rebel, African-American, Caucasian, Hispanic, etc., Baptist, Catholic, or Buddhist, Democrat, Republican, etc.

The more labels we use, the more we separate ourselves as Americans. I guess I'm more idealist than realist (okay, two more labels). I think most writers are. Nevertheless, idealistic dreams urge change and spur action. Look at what Martin Luther King accomplished because he had a dream.

AM: When did you first decide you were a writer?

RP: I've written as long as I can remember. I submitted my first short story to a magazine in 1972, just out of high school. Of course, I had no idea what I was doing. Submission guidelines? What are those?

My work, of course, was not successful, but the desire to write and submit never dwindled, so I never gave up. I pursued all the creative writing education I could afford while working and being a single mom for many years. I have file cabinets filled with handwritten poetry and typed (electric typewriter) short stories. In this way, I related to Eudora's determination, even though she never married and had children. She never let rejection kill her dream. I hope I never do either.

AM: Are you working on any projects now that our readers should know about?

RP: The History Press approached me about another book on Mississippi. This was after good friend and mentor author/artist Diane Williams asked me to co-author a book with her on the Depression in Mississippi. After submitting that idea to The History Press, our plans are to co-author both books for them.

Another project I'm excited about is for The University Press of Mississippi (UPM). UPM contacted my friend and incredible photographer, Glynn Fought, about a coffee-table book highlighting Mississippi cemeteries. He suggested that they include "stories behind the headstones." They were excited about the idea and Glynn contacted me about co-authoring this book with him. I'm excited about all these projects and working with two of the most talented artists I know!

AM: Thanks so much for this fascinating interview. All the best from all of us at *Southern Literary Review*.

RP: Thank you for all you do for Southern literature and authors!

Robert J. Ernst

APM: Thanks for taking the time to sit down for this interview, Bob. Your novel *The Inside War* is about an Appalachian mountain family during the Civil War. How long have you been interested in the Civil War?

RJE: I have had an interest in the Civil War for many years. Specifically, the effect of the war on Appalachia became an interest as I researched family history, now more than a decade ago. I realized that not much had been written, outside of academic treatises, on this aspect of the war. Bushwhacking ambushes, bands of roving deserters, intensely opposed partisan factions, and a breakdown in civil society befell western North Carolina. Of course, much study had been given to the poverty of the area during the twentieth century, but not much, save bluegrass music, about its culture. What I discovered was a vibrant pre-war society thoroughly rent by the war. And the area did not recover.

APM: The story of Will Roberts, your novel's protagonist, is similar to that of many actual soldiers who fought for the Confederacy. How much historical research went into this book? It seems as if there are a number of events in your story—Sammy Palmer's shooting of the sheriff, for instance—that track historical occurrences.

RJE: Much of the story is based on historical events. In fact, Will Roberts was a real person, as was his brother, Edwin. I traced their wartime adventures, researched the battles and conditions of their captivity and wove a fictional story around them. Likewise their wives, as portrayed in the story, were based on real people, although their story is more fictionalized. The novel does incorporate many historical characters and events that occurred in the vicinity of Marshall, North Carolina, by which I attempt to portray a picture of the character of the area and the severe impact of the war on it.

APM: There are some themes in the book that cover an aspect of the Civil War that is not often covered. Tell us about those.

RJE: The tactic of bushwhacking, or ambushing mountain patrols, is one. Guerrilla warfare as a matter of accepted tactics was new and was a terrifying degradation of the morality of warfare. There was a real cultural divide among the citizens of western North Carolina between those who supported the North, the "tories," and those who supported the Confederacy. These divisions played out in many ways, most notably in atrocities like the Shelton Laurel massacre, but more subtly in familial and neighbor relationships. I doubt many women suffered as did those in Appalachia, from the depredations, theft and physical threat of the men who populated the mountains during the war. I was surprised to learn of the inhumane prison conditions at Ft. Delaware. Everyone knows of Andersonville, but not many are aware of Ft. Delaware. We know of the great Civil War battles, but there were scores of skirmishes every week that terrified the contestants and shaped their perceptions. Certainly, Roberts's family suffered greatly, even though their war happened in the background to better known events.

APM: You seem careful not to glorify war but to present it as the complex tragedy that it is. The book's dedication states, "For those who have suffered war." I wonder if the process of writing this book taught you anything about war itself. What do you think?

RJE: The grand histories of the conflicts, eulogizing the fallen and celebrating the victorious are all necessary parts of our remembrance of a terrible, national conflict. What I found in researching this story was intense personal suffering, unnoted except at the basic unit of society, the family, and rippling out to the church, neighborhood and town. Why would a woman abandon her children? What would drive a member of the home guard to massacre captives – mere boys? How could people, so crushed, hope? And, of course, the main theme of *The Inside War* is hope; hope after, and despite the loss and suffering. As we deal with the veterans of the conflict with radical Islamists we need to surround them with a culture of hope.

APM: From one attorney to another, do you think being a lawyer affects your writing in any way—from the preparation to the organization to the style?

RJE: That's interesting. Certainly the actual practice of law involves clear writing. I have a hard time reading novels written in stream of consciousness or in rambling, shuffling styles. So, hopefully this book will be understandable and clear to the reader. I like the process of legal research and enjoyed the process of researching this book. However, the characters, though based on historical figures, came about from my imagination, which is why the book is a novel and not a history.

APM: It's been said that the Revolutionary War produced political philosophy in America whereas the Civil War produced literature. Do you agree with this, and if so, why?

RJE: Perhaps the truth in that statement devolves from the Revolutionary War defining the creation of a nation, the Civil War defining its character. The revolution tested the theories of individual liberty and melded them, free of sovereign control, imperfectly into a new nation. The Civil War represents a gigantic challenge to the notion that a nation of citizens can be free. Millions were intimately involved in the latter conflict and the upheaval and changes were intensely felt and recorded in innumerable books. But the fundamental story of both wars is ongoing, in my view, and that is America must re-experience "a new birth of freedom" with regularity if America is to retain her vibrancy and hope.

APM: Thanks, Bob, for taking the time. I appreciate it, and I know our readers do, too.

Barbara Davis

APM: *Through my fault.*
Through my fault.
Through my most grievous fault.
So opens your novel *The Wishing Tide*. This refrain is repeated elsewhere in the novel in chapters attributed to the character Mary. It's a rhythmic reminder, I think, of the crashing and retreating tides of love and life. What about this opening scene frames the rest of the book?

BD: I love that you picked up on the rhythm of those opening lines, and how they mimic the sea. I really wanted to establish the sea as a presence in the book, and liked the idea of the sea as both Mary's confessor, and the keeper of secrets. There's also the religious connotation of the lines from the old Catholic Confiteor, which, growing up with nuns, would have been drilled into Mary from an early age. One of the recurring themes in *The Wishing Tide,* for all the main characters, but especially for Mary, is the damage guilt can inflict, and the healing that only forgiveness can bring.

APM: You have a gift for prose and a talent for shaping characters. To a certain extent the former can't be learned or cultivated—some of it just comes naturally—but the latter, it seems to me, requires a lot of work. Would you mind explaining how you developed the three main characters in this book—Lane, Michael, and Mary? For instance, did you begin by outlining their traits, or did the characters just flow from mind to page and take shape as you worked?

BD: Mary came first, and was the product of a rather eccentric woman I met while walking along the cliff walk in Newport. She was at once forthcoming and evasive, telling me what she wanted me to know, but clearly withholding significant pieces of her life. Within an hour of that conversation's end I knew who Mary was, and what she'd been through. Lane and Michael both evolved more gradually, their traits and scars building as the story progressed and I got to know them and how they fit into Mary's story. I loved writing them all, but Mary was my linchpin.

APM: Tell us about your decision to alternate narrators from chapter to chapter.

BD: Each character in *Tide* is so unique, and, based on their life experiences, possess such different views of the world, that I felt the only way to truly convey them and their transformations was to let the reader see the world and events through their eyes. Also, there is knowledge each character has that none of the others possesses. Those bits of knowledge had to be carefully woven through the story in order for it to evolve naturally, and I hope, seamlessly. I especially wanted readers to be able to get inside Mary's head, to get a sense of how wounded she is, and yet how wise she can be in moments of clarity.

APM: Which narrator is your favorite? Whose perspective was the easiest to write from?

BD: Hands down, Mary was my favorite narrator in *Tide*. I love creating a distinct voice for these types of characters, a pattern and cadence that is distinctly theirs. It can be challenging, and usually takes three or four passes to get the flavor just right, but when I finally find it, it's so worth the work. The easiest narrator was definitely Lane. Parts of her character are a little autobiographical, so it felt easy to find her voice and share her take on the world.

APM: The coast can be a wistful setting, and a pensive one. What draws you to it?

BD: Personally, I've always been drawn to the sea, to its primal nature, its vastness and timelessness. And it's so deliciously tactile, a feast for every one of the senses when you think about it. But mostly, it feels like the perfect metaphor for life—turning and returning, giving and taking. It's a backdrop with a built-in pulse, which is pretty hard to beat.

APM: You state in the Acknowledgments section of your book that the "writer's journey is said to be a lonely one, but I never felt alone." This seems like a statement of fact, but could it also be a form of advice?

BD: I actually cried when I first wrote that line, because I don't think I realized how true it was until the words came off my fingertips. I've been so blessed to have support from so many wonderful people, both inside and outside of the literary world, and it's made all the difference in the world.

And yes, there *is* some advice there, and it's this: surround yourself with people who "get it," who get what you do, and why you do it. These are the people who will keep you sane, who will push you, and cheer you, and keep you moving on your own journey.

APM: Are you currently working on any projects that our readers will want to know about?

BD: My current work in progress is set on Florida's Gulf coast, on a pristine strip of beach called Hideaway Key. It's the story of Lily St. Claire, a young woman who inherits a beach cottage from her father, that neither she nor her mother even knew he owned. When Lily heads south to investigate, she finds boxes and boxes of memorabilia, all of it belonging to Lily-Mae Boyle, the infamously beautiful aunt whose name has been forbidden for as long as she can remember. As Lily sifts through journals and old scrapbooks, a story of betrayal and sibling rivalry gradually comes to light, painting a very different picture of the infamous Lily-Mae Boyle than the one her mother has been painting for years.

APM: Thank you so much for taking the time, Barbara. I'm wishing you much success with *The Wishing Tide*.

Jolina Petersheim

APM: Thanks for taking the time to talk to *Southern Literary Review*, Jolina. Your latest novel, *The Midwife*, follows closely on the heels of *The Outcast*. Did you expect these books to be the successes they've been?

JP: All authors dream that their novels will be successful, and I was certainly no exception. Still, I had no idea these two stories would resonate so deeply with readers. I have been moved almost to tears, time and time again, to hear a personal story about how these novels touched a reader's life. This means far more to me than best-seller status or critical acclaim. I am so grateful.

APM: I recently mentioned your book to a friend, who said she didn't know that "Amish literature was a thing." She was referring of course to genre. I suppose I didn't know this genre was as popular as it is, but it makes sense to me. There's a certain suspense to this way of life that we—many people I mean—no longer practice in our current culture. I'm reminded of Jane Austen: the pleasure of reading her books is heightened if you understand the mores and customs of the characters. What do you make of all this?

JP: With both of my novels, I try to go deeper than the quintessential Amish boy-meets-*Englischer* girl dilemma. I grew up on a Christian camp (or community) from the time I was six until I was fourteen, and during those eight years, I witnessed the elements that can bring a community together and tear it apart. Since I have a Mennonite heritage, it seemed natural to combine these two interests: the definition of community and the Mennonites. So far, the questions keep spinning entirely new plot threads. I just follow wherever they lead.

APM: Could you give our readers the premise of *The Midwife*?

JP: *The Midwife* is a story about a mother who risks everything to save a child not genetically hers. The concept of surrogacy was first brought to my attention when my dear friend in college discussed using a gestational surrogate in the future because she would be unable to carry a child of her own due to the medication she was taking for a heart transplant.

This made me contemplate all of the many obstacles in surrogacy that everyone involved would have to overcome:

What if the surrogate became attached to the child? What if, God forbid, something happened to one of the parents, or if there was a chromosomal abnormality, and the parents decided they did not want the child any longer?

All of these disparate ideas coalesced into the concept for *The Midwife* once I gave birth to a child of my own. I knew that even if I was of no relation to the child, if my body had sustained her for nine months, she would still be my daughter, even if we shared no genetic connection.

From there, the story went on to expound upon the heights and depths a mother will go to protect that child, and what is the definition of motherhood: genetics or love.

APM: There's a lot there—womanhood, motherhood, fertility. What draws you to these themes? Is there someone in the so-called literary canon from whom you draw inspiration or motivation?

JP: I don't believe I would've been able to write either of my stories without the perspective of being a mother. I was expecting our firstborn daughter when I wrote *The Outcast*—a modern retelling of *The Scarlet Letter* set in an Old Order Mennonite community in Tennessee—and she was only twelve weeks old when I began crafting *The Midwife*. It was a transformative experience to place myself in the midwife Rhoda's shoes and imagine my daughter being taken from me without any power to get her back. I actually miscarried during the editorial process of *The Midwife*, and it was beautiful and heart-wrenching to read back over the scenes my own fingers had typed and find such healing through the midwife's journey of overcoming loss and learning to love again. My prayer is that this story will touch my readers' lives to the same extent it did mine.

APM: Let's talk about you—Jolina the writer. In a sense we can never divorce our subjective self—the "I myself" whom Whitman celebrates—from our writing, but I'd like to know or to try to know who you are *as a writer*. Writing can be a very private and solitary activity—at least when the muse strikes. Writing almost always eventually becomes a collaborative activity, what with editors and proofreaders and the like. But the initial product is yours alone, a creature of the imagination. What makes you write what you write? Do you ever find yourself lost in a world of your own creation?

JP: Long before I knew how to read or write, I would sit on the front porch and try to make up stories. My parents inadvertently encouraged this because my father—a barn builder by trade—would pause in his labors to jot down lyrics on his 2 x 4 boards with a carpenter's pencil, and my mother would read excerpts from her novels to me like a bedtime story. We also didn't have a TV for the majority of my childhood, so once I learned how to read, I would bring stacks of books home from the library. This, naturally, developed into a love for writing. I attempted to write my first novel when I was in sixth grade, and I've been compelled to create in this vein ever since.

I do often get lost in a world of my own creation, but I have also found that it's necessary to continue working even when the inspiration isn't there. Oftentimes, just sitting down to write each day will force those creative juices to start flowing. Even if they only flow for the last half hour of a four-hour stretch, that last half hour is then when the magic happens. It's addicting!

APM: You don't shy away from the psychology of your characters. Why not?

JP: I've always been fascinated by our motivations, for good and for evil. I like to explore these motivations—these behaviors—through writing to better understand why people do what they do, even if they're fictional. I love how crafting a novel helps me understand myself and those around me.

APM: You and your husband have similar backgrounds. How long did it take the two of you to figure that out, and if I could push this question into two, what effect does your background have on your books?

JP: My husband and I met at a church mainly composed of ex-Amish and Mennonites, so it sure didn't take long to figure out that we share the same background. Before we even journeyed down to southern Tennessee, my father was in contact with my husband's grandfather, Amos Stoltzfus, who was kicked out of the Amish church when he was seventeen. He was the one who invited us to church and who made sure that our family got introduced to everyone.

Even if I didn't write "Amish fiction," I believe my background would still remain very evident in my books. The Pennsylvania Dutch heritage is just something you cannot shake, and the customs are being carried on in our own family, although we're often not aware of it. (For instance, I use certain PA Dutch phrases with my daughter like *brutzing, ferhoodled, redd up*, etc.)

APM: Thanks, Jolina. There's just one more question I want to ask you, and I already know the answer because I read it somewhere, but I find it to be compelling and inspiring and selfishly want it to be archived here in *Southern Literary Review*. The question is, how did you come to find an agent and publish your first book?

JP: I met my agent, Wes Yoder, at an author reading when I was 25,000 words into the first draft of my debut, *The Outcast*. He asked if he could read the portion of the manuscript I had completed. I was skeptical at first because I had no idea that he was an agent; I just knew that he was a writer. Once we cleared that up, I went home and started working like crazy. I sent the polished version to him one month later. He read the story on his way home from a book festival in Brazil and told me he thought the story had potential, so I began to write as quickly as I could. I was expecting our little girl at the time; therefore, I knew I had a narrow window in which to finish the manuscript. I completed *The Outcast* in six months, and Wes and I had a two-book publishing contract with Tyndale House when my firstborn daughter was 12 weeks old. She is now twenty-eight months, and I have her little sister on the way—who we're expecting to meet in September—and all I can say is that it has been a delightful, somewhat challenging, but always a rewarding journey!

APM: I appreciate your taking the time, Jolina, and wish you the best on all your future endeavors.

JP: Thank you for having me here, Allen!

JEFF HIGH

AM: Thank you for doing this interview, Jeff, and let me just say that I enjoyed your novel, which represents the best of literary fiction—Southern style. I'd like to jump right into the interview the way you jumped right into the opening scene of the book, the scene with the Code Blue and the seemingly supernatural revival of Hoot, a big fella who goes into a cardiac arrest. Why did you begin with this scene? My guess is, your decision had something to do with the title of the book that's drawn from Hamlet's line: "There are more things in heaven and earth, Horatio, than are dreamt of in your philosophy." Might there have been more things in Watervalley than your medically trained protagonist could have dreamt of in his Vanderbilt schooling?

JH: Your question points to a central theme in the book. While clearly *More Things in Heaven and Earth* can be enjoyed on the surface as light-hearted fiction, there are some definitive thematic and theological elements working in the substrata. Some reviews have endeavored to pigeonhole the work as "feel good" fiction. Certainly, it has that quality. But I am delighted that *Southern Literary Review* has insightfully noticed the powerful themes that are subtly and regularly earmarked in the language. As an example, in the opening pages, Luke Bradford, as the narrator, makes the statement, "So in the back of your head is this scared whisper nagging at you, reminding you that you will make the difference between some guy staying alive and an awkward conversation with the family about how 'it was just his time.'"

The words "reminding you that you will make the difference" understate Luke's assumption that he is the center of the universe…it is he who brings order to the world. At least, so he thinks, at the first of the novel. However, Hoot's miraculous turnaround had nothing to do with Luke, and he, Luke, knows it. He acknowledges this when he states, "But this is Watervalley, and things like a Code Blue happen differently. They don't follow the normal order."

This sets in motion the underlying conflict that Luke wrestles with the entire story. The resolution of this occurs in the final chapter where he states, "At that moment I fully realized the importance of my life here. There was a larger agenda at work in the town that transcended my small plans and gave my life here a significance it would not otherwise have." For Luke, this is the "more things in heaven and earth" revelation. The language in the novel continuously speaks to the themes of "order versus disorder" and "darkness versus light."

As an example, Connie Thompson and John Harris are emblematic of the influences of light and darkness on Luke's journey. This is not so subtly revealed as John gives Luke an apple on their first encounter. As well, Connie appears judgmental at first. But eventually the story reveals that she is actually an endless wellspring of love and strength. In the end, John's self-made world is crumbling, and he longs to be close to the distant lights of Watervalley. Conversely, Connie is the enduring force, the permeating glue that holds Luke's world and the world of Watervalley together. If the reader is mindful of these thematic drivers and how they echo the internal conflict of Luke's journey, they provide for an enriched reading experience.

On a side note, the Hoot Wilson episode is based on a true story from my medical experience. Hospital staff coded this guy in his ICU room for a half hour, all to no avail. He was flat-line dead. Afterwards, his family was allowed in the room and his daughter squeezed his foot and told him not to go yet. That man is alive today. It still gives me chills when I think about it.

AM: That gives me chills as well, and the good kind. I'm curious about your decision to include a prelude and

postlude that, it seems, are from the perspective of some omniscient, third-person narrator. The rest of the book, of course, is from the perspective of Luke Bradford, a young doctor who has given up big dreams to move to Watervalley to pay off $200,000 in student debt. When and why did you decide to include the prelude and postlude?

JH: The prelude and postlude were part of the original concept of the book. The intention of the prelude was to trace the journey of something as insignificant as a single drop of water. Thus, the prelude poses the simple question: Is this world random or is there a larger order that animates the universe?

Clearly, the drop of water is allegorical for the journey of Luke Bradford. This is particularly notable in the phrases "it is cleansed from the impurities of the world behind" and "but time and pressure pull it downward toward the valley." Luke's trials are part of his cleansing, his sanctification, if you will. And the effect of "time and pressure" underscores the larger plan into which his life is inevitably drawn.

The postlude brings the drop of water metaphor full circle. Luke is now at peace with his place in the world and understands his role in the larger tapestry of life in Watervalley. At journey's end, he finds himself moved and consoled. Appropriately, the final sentence in the book shows him in a supplicant posture, looking up to the heavens with an upturned palm. He is holding a snowflake, a unique creation that is emblematic of Luke's unique life, his unique pilgrimage. Warmed by his touch, it now turns into a drop of water.

AM: That is a beautiful image. Let's forget, for just a minute, what the no-longer-new New Critics said almost a century ago. How much of your background—Southern, medical, educational—made its way into the novel in some form or another? Is there a little bit of Jeff High inside Luke Bradford?

JH: Being a son of the South and an RN definitely informed the story, but the novel is truly not autobiographical. My family has always placed great value on education. My mother was Valedictorian of her high school class, my father had a Ph.D. in genetics, my three brothers include a physician, a tax-lawyer, and a veterinarian, and I have degrees in English and nursing. Altogether, we have more degrees than Fahrenheit.

I probably do share some of the introvert tendencies of Luke Bradford, but the real confession is that John Horatio Harris is most likely a close alter ego. (My initials are JHH.) I tend to be an optimist. However, I also have those days where I can be rather cynical, and the voice of John Harris seems to pour out naturally.

AM: Elsewhere you have said that Connie Thompson is your favorite character in the book. Would you say more about that?

JH: The beautiful thing about Connie Thompson is that the reader is completely convinced that she is the real thing. Even if you have absolutely no use for Christianity and organized church, you still love her. You love her because she lives out her convictions of service and humility without ever being anybody's fool. And also, she just gets to say the best lines.

AM: ***More Things in Heaven and Earth*** **is the first in a series. Do you see Watervalley, the so-called "dropping-off point of God and all creation," as your own little Yoknapatawpha? What might we expect for the future of this town?**

JH: Watervalley provides a unique microcosm from which I have a long, long list of stories to tell. I highly suspect there will be several more books about Luke Bradford, but there is also a great opportunity down the road to tell fascinating back-stories, especially about the lives of John Harris and Connie Thompson. In the pages ahead, there will be a new owner of the Society Hill Bed and Breakfast who comes to town with her teenager. She will make an appearance in my next book, *Each Shining Hour*, and I suspect there will be some stories to tell about her experiences. I intend to write about Watervalley for many, many years.

AM: I'm sure that comes as good news to readers of this first installment. Okay, one last question. All authors struggle to see their manuscript through to print. There's the process of writing and revising, of seeking out the opinions of friends and colleagues, of finding an agent and editor, and so on. I'll put a broad question to you: What was it all like? How did you cope? What might you recommend to readers who are at that stage?

JH: I am convinced that my arrival as a published author was ecclesiastical, involving what appeared to be chance, but actually happening in the fullness of time. For over three decades I quietly wrote stories, read voraciously, and daydreamed about being published. But I never sought publication until I had written *More Things in Heaven and Earth*. This was the first work in which I seriously pursued an agent and publisher. I was fortunate. Attaining a contract happened within a few months.

It was a good piece of writing, but it was made infinitely better by my editor, Ellen Edwards at Penguin. Look, I'm a Southern boy. And I never would have guessed that a tough and talented Connecticut Yankee, my editor, would be the key to bringing my tales of small town Southern life to print. But thankfully, she saw a spark of possibility in the early manuscript and has been invaluable in the refinement of the story.

My advice to anyone seeking publication is threefold. Write about what you know; write about what you believe; and then rewrite it. I am an incurable revisionist. I constantly edit, redo, and rewrite, looking for that perfect word, that perfect sentence. I casually wrote for three decades before I thought I had something worthy of casting my bread upon the water.

Once you have done this, it is wise to network. Although it can be painful, you have to put yourself out there and tell your story. I realize that this advice comes as no big revelation. But then again, as I mentioned earlier, much about writing is ecclesiastical; there's nothing new under the sun. But there are always new stories to tell about the enduring truths of the human experience.

AM: Amen to that. Thank you again, Jeff, for taking the time. ***Southern Literary Review*** **looks forward to more work from you.**

JH: And thank you, so very much, for this opportunity.

David Bradley

AM: Thanks for doing this interview on the occasion of the ebook release of your 1981 novel, *The Chaneysville Incident*. It's been 32 years since the novel was first published. Does it speak differently to today's audience than it did upon its initial release?

DB: Thanks for the opportunity.

No writer really knows what a book, a novel, says to an audience. That's pretty much up to the audience. I would hope that there are a lot of things that were "news" in 1981, like a greater and more accurate sense of what slavery was all about, and what the Underground Railroad was all about, that are no longer surprising to as many readers. *The Chaneysville Incident* was shaped by a frustration with the assumptions and dominant theories of American History in the 1960s and 1970s—to put it simply, that black Americans had no history apart from the oppressions visited upon them by dominant American (which was to say, white) society—slavery, lynching, segregation, all sorts of racial discriminations.

At that time, most American historians, and the American History Establishment in general, approached the phenomena of racial oppression using as data only those documents—official records, minutes, laws, pamphlets, books, letters, personal diaries—created by white Americans who had promoted, countenanced, witnessed or opposed the oppressions. In terms of slavery, whether the author was a Southern plantation owner or a Northern abolitionist, what was "known" about slavery was what white Americans perceived and recorded—or wanted to perceive and record. But while historians gave great credence to these documents, the records and witnesses of the oppressed were ignored or dismissed as "unreliable" or "unauthentic." Historians knew a lot about what had been done and by whom it had been done and by whom it had been opposed, but they did not know—or often seemed not to care what it felt like or even looked like from the perspective of the oppressed. The inner life of black Americans was...*terra incognita.*

The result was a lopsided sense American history in which black Americans appeared not as historical actors but as historical objects, without personal stories and everyday lives and behavior that were shaped by free will or personal failings. Which meant that the oppressed—slaves, mulatto children, lynching victims—were inevitably seen as stereotypes, and those stereotypes were passed into the larger culture in books, plays, eventually movies, radio and television. The general perception of black Americans was that they were and could be, at most, bit players in the American drama, with no lines to speak other than, "Yes, sir."

This historical paradigm started to break down in the mid-1950s, in part because of more imaginative historical research, but also because images of black Americans who were definitely not bit players forced their way into the American consciousness. Black Americans were suddenly *visible* not only as victims but as protestors. That visibility had a lot to do with television coverage, which put those images of black Americans in the homes of white Americans where an actual black American was unlikely to set foot, except, perhaps, as a servant.

We've just celebrated the fiftieth anniversary of the March on Washington, which, whatever else it did or didn't do, made it absolutely impossible for white Americans to ignore the existence of black Americans. Which is not to say the stereotypes were dispelled; in terms of history and even in terms of current events the lives—not just the social conditions, but the inner emotional and spiritual lives—of black Americans were still *terra incognita* from the perspective of white America. But what was demonstrated powerfully on that day was that there was *something* there to know, that the people who lived there had thoughts and...well, dreams. Now, perhaps, it seems obvious. But in 1963, that a black man dreamed *anything* was news. A lot of White Americans hadn't even thought about what black Americans dreamed.

Sorry. Didn't mean to give a history lecture. But part of the "mission" of the *Chaneysville Incident* (and also of my earlier novel *South Street,* although in a different way) was to present the inner lives of black Americans as they deal with those phenomena of oppression. To my mind the best way to reveal the interior lives of people is to let them talk while the reader listens. John Washington is a first-person narrator, but he doesn't actually tell the story; it comes to him in bits and pieces, from documents and narratives and observations. One reason John is an historian is that he does research, which means he doesn't talk; he listens to a lot of other people talk. As an historian, John is outside the experience. But as a black American he is inside. He has been exempted from the most obvious oppressions—slavery, lynching, educational discrimination, employment discrimination, housing discrimination. He can live where he wants, love, even marry, whom he wants. But his personal narrative is not a discrete story; it is the culmination of a long line of narratives; his life the visible end of a sequence of oppressive experiences. And the question is, what is he going to do about it? Is he going to let the past destroy the possibilities of his present?

But to answer your question directly: If you'd asked me in 1981 or '82, I would have said I'd hope that by 2013 much of the historical information that I had to include so readers would understand what was going on would be common knowledge—for example, that "modern" American readers would understand that there was no such thing as "free territory" south of Canada, that the Ku Klux Klan and lynching were not purely Southern phenomena. And I would have hoped that a person like John Washington would be fundamentally less foreign—a black man with a Ph.D. in history who is a professor at a major university and who studies not slavery, per se, but international atrocities and who teaches courses not in "Afro-American History" but in the Civil War. I would have said I'd hope by now such things would be commonplace.

That doesn't seem to be the case. It seems the actual understanding of how race works in America hasn't progressed that far. The rhetoric has developed, that's for sure. The worst legal practices and social customs of the 1950s and 1960s have surely been altered. And I suppose that the presidency of Barack Obama does mean something—although in terms of culture, I don't know that it really means that much. But I don't think we Americans understand the mechanisms of our history better than we did in 1981, and we certainly don't understand each other any better. For example, racial incidents, especially those involving the police, are often presented as "isolated incidents."

White Americans tend to accept that characterization and to see the responses of black Americans as irrationally angry, even paranoid. But most black Americans do not accept that those incidents are isolated. They see them as connected to patterns that have been repeated time and again throughout American history. My point is not who's right and who's wrong; it's that white Americans tend not to understand why black Americans are reacting as they do because the white Americans are not aware of the history. Recently, I was speaking with a thirty-something white woman, born and raised in Chicago, about something... cultural. It turned out that she'd never heard of the Emmitt Till Case, despite the Chicago connection. She's not stupid, she's not racist, she's a good friend. She just... wasn't aware of a piece of history, which is itself connected to a lot of other pieces of history, that creates a cultural awareness that influences the social and political responses of black people in her city. Basically, she doesn't know where they're coming from.

So, I think the novel still has work to do. Because it talks about why black people do things that might seem...strange. Like killing their husbands...

AM: I would venture to guess that all writers have had the strange experience of rereading their work years later only to find that the prose seems to have been written by someone else, or at least is not so familiar that the eye runs over words because the mind knows what's coming next. Do you ever find yourself rereading the book and seeing in it a voice—or at least a turn of phrase—that no longer

seems a product of your own mind?

DB: No, because I don't reread the book. Never have read it. I've read sections from it to audiences, and I've had the eerie experience of hearing people talk about it. The last time was a class of graduate literature students who kept going on about the rape scene. I'm sitting there going to myself, "Did you write a rape scene? I don't remember a rape scene." I had to go back and check. Turned out I remembered right. No rape scene. A confession scene. But in general, I don't reread what I write once it's been published. Every time I do, I end up doing a new draft...even if it's too late.

AM: In 1988, Klaus Ensslen reviewed *The Chaneysville Incident* in *Callaloo* and claimed that you had "presented a narrative text in which authenticated historical material is so charged with the expressive claims of fiction as symbolic action that the book may today already claim a unique position within Afro-American fiction—a narrative tradition well-known for its concern with history." This comment raises several questions, but I want to focus on its implied suggestion that you were doing something new based on something old—namely, on history itself. How do you think this suggestion stands up to the test of time? If I could add to that, how would you categorize the novel in light of what has come before and after it?

DB: I didn't do anything new. Far from it. I learned how to do it by reading—studying, in fact—William Faulkner's *Absalom, Absalom!* and Robert Penn Warren's *All the King's Men* and Shirley Ann Grau's *The Keepers of the House*. Also Daniel DeFoe's *Journal of the Plague Year*. Also William Shakespeare's...

Don't get me wrong. I'm really happy with that "charged with the expressive claims of fiction as symbolic action." That's what I was trying to do. But...I stole so many of the ideas and mechanisms. For John Washington and Judith Powell, read Quentin Compson and Shreve MacKenzie.

AM: So much has been said and written about the blurring of fact and fiction, not just in this novel but in all works of fiction, that I'm hesitant to ask for your take in such a brief interview—and no doubt you've been asked

more times than you can remember—but *The Chaneysville Incident* seems to cry out for an explanation. There is always something to be said for a work of fiction that undertakes the subject of history, since the connection between those genres is not intuitive, and the complex interplay between fact and fiction seems so much more provocative and revealing and powerful in the context of race in this country. Can you speak to this aspect of the novel? It's such an interesting issue now as the novel itself becomes "canonized" as part of history.

DB: You didn't say this was supposed to be a short interview. And here I've been going on and on. Sorry. But…ask a novelist a question…

First of all, there's history and there's historiography. History is what happened. Historiography is what some author has written about it to try to report or explain or contextualize what happened. But what's written is never what happened. No historiographer, not even an eye-witness—maybe especially not an eye-witness—has all the facts. All historiographers have a point of view or acquire one in the course of research. Some historiographers flat-out lie, some are deluded or biased. Even the most responsible can't get it all right. It drives them crazy. That's why John Washington dreams about Historian's Heaven.

Novelists don't care if it's all right in terms of what happened. Some care less than others. My preference is to get as much right as I can, but that may be because I'm lazy—it's a lot easier to start with a template, like a town, or a cast of characters or an historical event—and invent within it, than start from scratch.

But I do think it's important that fiction that deals with "controversial" aspects of American history be able to withstand a certain kind of scrutiny, because there are so many Americans determined to disbelieve. But facts are hard to dismiss, and corroboration is important; people have made "pilgrimages" to Chaneysville, Pennsylvania to see the graveyard where the slaves are buried—I'm not sure why, except I guess it makes the novel seem more real to them, which is actually a strange thing to say about a novel. But if I'd made it up those people wouldn't have gotten what they wanted, maybe what they needed to make the fiction work for them.

You can understand why. Nobody *wants* to think about five thousand people showing up to see a black man tortured, hanged and burned. Nobody in their right mind *wants* to believe stuff like that. I don't myself. A lot of what I did in *The Chaneysvlle Incident* was actually avoidance of the worst and most complicated atrocities. Enough was enough. Atrocity was John Washington's thing. Not mine.

But what I learned (the hard way; well, actually, I learned from reading Richard Wright, but I came to believe it the hard way) is that when it comes to race in America, fiction is too easy to dismiss. Also, historical truth is sometimes so complicated and horrible that it gets in the way of the narrative; a lot of what I did in *The Chaneysvlle Incident* was to avoid the worst and most complicated atrocities. That's John Washington's thing. Not mine.

But since *The Chaneysville Incident,* most of what I've written has been creative non-fiction, because I got tired of people saying, "Well, that's just fiction. He made it up." The truth was, I toned it down, because history is often…unbelievable. Sometimes it's unbelievably funny. But some people say I have a sick sense of humor.

Last part of your question: I believe every work of literature is a part of a nation's cultural history. Somebody wrote it, and somebody—maybe not a lot of people, maybe not the college professors, but somebody—read it. Sometimes it had social impact, like *The Klansman* or *The Jungle* or *Native Son*. Sometimes the effect is more covert, as with *Stranger in a Strange Land* or *The Turner Diaries*. There's always a lot of important writing that isn't canonized.

AM: As a professor of creative writing, do you feel that there are certain things that cannot be taught? Is there any particular piece of advice—your "signature" piece of advice, let's call it—that you give students?

DB: Quit. Seriously. I tell them to quit. If they can. And if they can, it's nothing to be ashamed of. But if they can't quit, and they don't care, they don't want to work, they just want to bang on the keyboard all day, I say welcome to the club…and don't blame it on me.

Actually, I think of myself less as a teacher (and certainly not a professor) of writing than as a coach. And as any coach will tell you, the one thing you can't create is desire. But given desire, there's almost nothing about writing that can't be learned. There is a lot that can't be taught, because it's based on personal vision. But there's a great deal that can be presented and, if properly presented, learned.

First lesson: sit alone in a room for a day and don't talk to anybody except yourself and people you are making up.

Second Lesson: Repeat.

Third Lesson: After five days, ask yourself if you're eager for day six.

AM: Are you working on any projects now that might interest readers of *Southern Literary Review*?

DB: For many years I have been working on a book called *The Bondage Hypothesis: Meditations on Race, History and America*. I'm not sure it will interest anybody, frankly, but it might interest people who want to know why, although our fathers brought forth on this continent a new nation dedicated to the proposition that all are created equal, eleven score and seventeen years later we still haven't gotten it right. Part of the reason—much of the reason—has to do with the historical process that inspired *The Chaneysville Incident*. I think it's almost finished. But I said that four years ago.

I've also returned to fiction. I'm working on a collection of stories set in what I call "the Town" in *The Chaneysville Incident*. Now it's called Raystown. One of the stories "You Remember the Pinmill" was published a year or so ago in *Narrative*. Which I like because it's (a) online and (b) free.

AM: Thanks so much for taking the time, David. It's been an honor.

DB: Thank you, and not only for this interview. Your reviews are first rate, and I've picked up on a number of new-to-me writers from your website. Like I said, there's always a lot of important writing that isn't canonized. Thanks for clueing me in to some.

Jessica Dotta

AM: Congratulations on your forthcoming trilogy, Jessica, and thanks for talking about it with me. Just because your books are set in England doesn't mean you're not a Southern author, right? Why don't we begin with some publicity: tell us about your debut novel—and the whole trilogy for that matter.

JD: Thank you so much, Allen! I really appreciate your taking time to interview me.

The Price of Privilege trilogy is set in Victorian England and is narrated by the protagonist Julia Elliston, who after a lifetime of silence has decided to set the record straight about the great scandal she caused in her teens.

Born of Persuasion begins the account with seventeen-year-old Julia. She's recently orphaned and living on the charity of an anonymous guardian who intends to establish her as a servant in far-off Scotland. She has two months to devise a better plan.

Her first choice, to marry her childhood sweetheart, is denied when she discovers he's made a change of faith. But when a titled dowager offers to introduce Julia into society, a realm of possibilities opens. Treachery and deception, however, are as much a part of Victorian society as titles and decorum, and Julia quickly discovers her present is deeply entangled with her mother's mysterious past. With no laws to protect her, she must unravel the secrets on her own.

AM: I'm curious: how did the trilogy come about? Or is it still in the works? In other words, did you set out to write

a trilogy, or was your book so long that someone advised you to separate it into divisions?

JD: It started with a single scene I penned in my teens. I had just finished *Jane Eyre* and was wild with enthusiasm at its singular style and storyline. It was the first novel where I couldn't predict the ending and therefore I felt unsafe. I lost two nights' sleep, turning pages, wondering what would happen. I had no idea stories could be that wild and free. That scene is the opening to Chapter Ten.

From there, the story just plain haunted me. The scene raised interesting questions, and I wanted to know why the characters were acting the way they were. They were awful. It also revealed a lot about my protagonist's past, and I wanted answers to those questions, as well.

When I finally started writing, I only had planned up to the most devastating moment in the novel. As I began to write the aftermath, it turned into Book Two, with its own complete set of problems.

I had 400K written with a plan for Book Three.

So I divided what I had into two books and labored to bring each of those 200K words into a 100-130K word story. In some ways, the characters are deeper because of this process—I know more about them than I can possibly put into a novel. Other times, I've had to go back and forth with Tyndale's amazing editing team, in order to make the motivation of the character clearer or explain how it ties into the story. I cut a lot of scenes and choosing the ones that needed to stay isn't easy.

AM: ***Downton Abbey*** **is quite the television series. Your books will appeal to the audience of that series. What is it about this Edwardian period and British genre that appeals to Americans? William Deresiewicz refers to this phenomenon as "America's love affair with the English aristocracy." Why this love affair?**

JD: Love this question! I think to do it justice I need to answer it in parts. As far as English aristocracy—how can we not have a fascination? If Britain is our distant cousin, then its aristocracy is our elegant yet condescending aunt, who once visited and left behind an indelible impression.

Yet, I don't fully agree with Mr. Deresicwicz that the fascination stays strictly within aristocracy. We love to follow the Grantham family, particularly the dowager countess, but what makes us adore Downton Abbey is the staff. What would the show be without Carson's high standards, Bates' dignity or Daisy's struggle for equality?

Why does the Edwardian era particularly seem to fascinate? I believe it's because the changes wrought during that period are still affecting us today. On this side of history, we can watch the stories unfold with a sense of standing on the moral high ground. Should a maid be allowed to better her life by becoming a secretary? Of course, we cry, as we watch the rest of society frown upon her for daring to question convention. We know for whom we're rooting. We're cheering for our own value system.

It grows more difficult when one dips into other eras. There are completely foreign values at play as we follow the characters' struggles. In this case, the writer's job is to ensure that the reader understands the restraints of the era. When they do, stories from other eras dazzle as well. The Tudor period of history is a good example of this. King Henry VIII's court is alive and well today. You'd be surprised how well the modern woman can debate whether Anne Boleyn was a huntress or a victim. Authors like Philippa Gregory have done an outstanding job making that society come alive. No one reads her books and wonders why Jane Seymour didn't refuse the King's attention. They are fully aware of the consequences she would reap.

AM: Do you share this love affair?

JD: Yes, I do. I love the Regency, Victorian, and Edwardian eras, but with eyes wide open.

While I love the elegance of each era—the charm of tea, lawn parties, and bustling gowns, I am not fooled into wishing I was born during that period. My parents are laborers, and as such, I would have been lucky to gain employment as a scullery maid, and they had the cruelest workload. I have several friends who would have died in childbirth. My own daughter wouldn't have survived long. I've taken several trips to the ER in the middle of the night for acute croup. Right now, I share custody of my daughter, but in the Regency and Victorian eras, I would have had no legal right to even visit her. Fathers automatically had sole custody of children in a divorce. (Not that divorces could be obtained except by an act of Parliament.)

When one understands the precariousness of women in that time period, it makes wonderful drama, but I wouldn't want to have lived there.

Much better to buy *Downton Abbey*-inspired clothing, host a tea party for friends, and then slip back into your jeans and modern life.

AM: Julia Elliston. Let's talk about her. She's your protagonist. Where did she come from? I don't mean her background or biography in the novel—I mean as a product of your imagination. How and why did you create her?

JD: Julia Elliston is not an average protagonist. Her characterization receives polar reactions from readers. Some find her unlikable, some humorous, and others think her isolation is heartbreaking.

We don't always know what we're writing until we've finished, and it is so with Julia. From the very beginning of the novel I "allowed" Julia to steer the story so to speak, without trying to soften her. (Actually, I couldn't if I wanted to. I developed writer's block every time I attempted to write her differently.)

Looking back, I see that I was exploring my own coming-of-age difficulties. I grew up in a household with very strict views on women and their roles. I have been complimented many times on my ability to bring the reader into the Victorian mindset, but the truth is I was brought up under that mindset; therefore, it is not difficult for me to capture.

AM: This is your debut work. *Southern Literary Review* receives emails from aspiring writers all the time. We get questions about conferences and workshops, about authors and writing communities. Our readers always seem to be curious about how they can produce their first work. What advice do you have for these readers—any words of encouragement?

JD: Attend writer conferences, network, and never give up. But I know everybody says that, so with the disclaimer that it really is the best advice I can give, here's what I suggest to writers

I've critiqued or mentored.

1. Go to the The Gutenberg Project, download and work through *The Century Handbook of Writing* by Garland Greever and Easley S. Jones. Better yet, team up with another writer and pledge to work through it together, ensuring you really learn its concepts.

2. Read books that make you despair of ever writing as well as those authors.

3. Learn as much about the publishing industry as possible. Many feel that once they're offered a contract, their work is done. That's only true if they don't plan to publish again, or are very, very lucky. There's as much work after publication as there is prior to it.

4. When discouraged, read *For The Young Who Want To* by Marge Piercy. It will help on your worst days.

5. Set up a fun routine for rejection letters. I used to sing "Another One Bites the Dust" as I filed the newest rejection. It cheered me.

AM: Thanks for taking the time, Jessica. We at *Southern Literary Review* wish you the best and look forward to the publication of your trilogy.

JD: Thank you so much for inviting me!

Karen White

AM: Thank you so much, Karen, for taking time out of your busy schedule to do this interview with *Southern Literary Review*. We're excited about the release of your new book, *The Time Between*. You've said that this book might be your favorite so far. Why is that?

KW: I think that with each book I grow as a writer. This book has more complex characters and plot lines than I've ever done before. I "stretched my writing legs" with this book and I'm really proud of the results.

AM: The story is set, for the most part, on Edisto Island and in Charleston, South Carolina. How did you choose this setting? If I may, I'll add this question to that one: the backdrop of Hungary during WWII—where did you get the idea for that?

KW: I love the South Carolina Lowcountry and have set the majority of my books there (including a series of four books set in Charleston). I chose Hungary for the WWII element of the story because of its unique position during the war as an Axis ally. The Hungarian government at the time hated the Nazi regime, but they hated the Soviet Communists more, and found themselves stuck between a rock and a hard place for much of the war. However, because its Jewish citizens were protected by some extent by their own government, Hungary became a refuge to Jews fleeing from Nazi-occupied European countries. This all changed in two short months in 1944—which became the crux of my story.

AM: I think it was Hemingway who said that there is nothing to write because all you do is sit down at the typewriter—or, in our era, the computer—and bleed. In what ways, if at all, did this story "bleed" out of you?

KW: This book is very emotional on many levels—all the characters have experienced some sort of tragedy in their lives and have had to find a way to move on. I'm very much like an actress who "becomes" her characters, and I immersed myself in Helena's and Eleanor's complicated lives and emotions. It was exhausting, and after a day of writing I could barely speak!

AM: Everyone is necessarily bound to understand the world through his or her own experiences, and I always want to know how those experiences shape the stories authors write. How has your experience influenced this novel? I don't mean to suggest that your biography is somehow plugged into the text but to find out whether and how certain personal experiences affected what did or did not make it into the text?

KW: I think in the beginning of an author's career, there are much more autobiographical elements in their work. However, as much of their personal issues are expressed in each subsequent work, the author is allowed to delve into other fictional lives as their career progresses. *The Time Between* is my 17th novel, so a lot of my "childhood angst" has pretty much been played out in my earlier works. Apparently, my disappointment at having never been given a sister (I was raised with three brothers) continues to play itself out in my novels! There are two sets of sisters at the heart of *The Time Between*. I think I will never tire of exploring this very complex family relationship in my fiction, most of it derived from listening to my mother and her sisters (all five of them!) talking over my grandmother's kitchen table late into the night when they didn't know I was listening.

AM: Two themes emerge in this story: family and memory. Everyone can relate to these. Do you find it challenging to undertake these themes in a new or different way—that is, in a way that people can understand based on their own experiences but also that is far enough removed from those experiences that it exercises readers' imagination?

KW: I get asked this question a lot, mostly because my novels usually center around family and dark secrets from the past. I think I get a fresh perspective on this with every book because with each novel I write, the characters are unique to me (and my readers), with different backgrounds, perspectives, values, and pasts. I use my characters to tell me their story—instead of me forcing them into a pre-planned scenario—which makes my themes of family and memory new and exciting with each book.

AM: How do you stay so productive?

KW: I don't believe in writer's block! There are many, many times I don't feel like sitting down and writing, but deadlines never go away. I'm a big believer in writing anyway—it's *always* easier to fix a bad page than stare at a blank page. That's my motto.

AM: Thank you again for taking the time to do this interview. I hope all of our readers will add *The Time Between* to their summer reading list.

KW: Thank you!

Lauren Clark

AM: Lauren, thank you for doing this interview. I'm glad to have the opportunity to ask you about *Dancing Naked in Dixie*. Before I get to the book, though, I'd like to ask you about your transition from television to writing. How did that transition take place?

LC: I loved working in TV news and it was great when my son was little. I worked for two different CBS stations—first anchoring the weekend news and then the morning news in Dothan, Alabama. The shift was 2 am to 10 am, so after three years, I needed a change and a regular schedule. I then took a job in pharmaceutical sales, but was able to transition into stay-at-home mom and full-time writer soon after. It's what I've always wanted to do as a career.

AM: Okay, on to *Dancing Naked in Dixie*. The protagonist of the book is Julia Sullivan. Tell us about her. What was the impetus behind this character? Did you develop her in stages, or did you have some preconceived notion of her character that you wanted to realize in the text?

LC: Fortunately, Julia Sullivan came to the pages of *Dixie* almost fully formed. She is a well-traveled writer, perpetually busy, and married to her job—largely to avoid dealing with her mother's death, her boyfriend, and a painful estrangement from her father. She's talented, with personality—but definitely has an ADHD side that gets her into some trouble when she acts before she thinks.

There's a lot of me in Julia—especially since I made the move from New York to Alabama twelve years ago. Many of her experiences (sweet tea, fire ants) are based on my experiences.

Julia was developed with change in mind. I wanted her out of her comfort zone, in a totally new environment that she'd decided to dislike. Much of *Dixie* involves Julia discovering secrets about her parents' relationship and realizing that forgiveness isn't as frightening as she believes.

AM: Within the last month, I've become an Alabamian, and I grew up taking family vacations to Destin, Florida, by way of Eufaula, Alabama, so I'm interested in the role that Eufaula plays in *Dancing Naked in Dixie*. Why Eufaula? What made you choose this city?

LC: Eufaula is my favorite Alabama city. When I was an anchor at WTVY in Dothan, I loved driving up on the weekends and having a light lunch, stopping at Shorter Mansion, and browsing in the lovely gift shops. Lake Eufaula is nearby, and on my trips to Atlanta, I would often stop at the state park to take in the beautiful, calming scenery.

I've attended the Pilgrimage several times, but it was during one of the candlelight tours, with everyone in antebellum costume, that I decided Eufaula provided that bit of magic that would make it the perfect setting for a story.

AM: Julia is, you could say, a cosmopolitan jetsetter who, due to events largely out of her control, finds herself living and working in Alabama. Do you think the South is indispensable to your writing? In other words, could the narrative in *Dancing Naked in Dixie* have transpired in some other geographical area? If not, why not?

LC: The South is indispensable to *Dixie*, and all of my books, to some extent, have Southern ties. Julia's story—her cosmopolitan edge and big city sharpness—had to be balanced out with the warm and loving nature of the Deep South. It became the perfect balance to round out her empty life, the yin to her yang.

I am sure that many talented writers could place the story with a "Julia" character traveling from the majestic Pacific Northwest to the warmth of New Mexico or Arizona, but I prefer to write from experience and draw on the sights and sounds that I know and love. For me, there's a certain charm about the Deep South that can't be duplicated.

AM: Thank you for taking the time, Lauren. I wish you all the best.

Julia Nunnally Duncan

AM: **Thank you for taking the time to do this interview, and congratulations on your forthcoming book,** *Barefoot in the Snow***. This is, I believe, your third collection of poetry. How does this one differ from your earlier books of poetry?**

JND: *Barefoot in the Snow* reflects a more mature vision and perspective of events and people because these poems were mostly written in the past two or three years. Some poems in this collection, such as "His Hands" and "My Uncle's Grave," took a longer time to germinate and more courage to share. I can't imagine having tackled these poems earlier in my life.

AM: **T.S. Eliot once said that genuine poetry can communicate before it is understood. Do you try to communicate with readers, or do you write for yourself? The answer to that is probably both, so let me rephrase the question this way: do you have a particular audience in mind as you write poetry, or are you more consumed with the craft, with "getting it right," so to speak?**

JND: Unless I am writing for a specific magazine theme or contest, such as the poem "My Mother's Elm" that I wrote to submit to the Joyce Kilmer Poetry Contest (and for which I was thankfully named a winner), I write only with the intention of composing the most honest and polished piece I can. But even with "My Mother's Elm," the poem took over once I started it, and I forgot the contest until I finished it. My goal was, most importantly, to capture a particular tree's place in my childhood and to select my most poignant associations with the tree.

AM: **Why do you write poetry?**

JND: To capture memories, to record reflections, and to work out intellectual and psychological puzzles and give them tangible form that others might recognize and be moved by.

AM: You have written in a variety of genres. Which comes easiest for you?

JND: A poem is easiest because, in general, it takes shape and is completed more quickly than a short story, an essay, or a novel. I have also discovered that my poems tend to find a readership more quickly too. My novels might have garnered me wider recognition and usually more regional response, but poems have allowed me more comfortable expression of what's in my heart.

AM: Do you find that poetry demands a certain economy of language that sets it apart from other forms of writing?

JND: By the nature of the poetic form—the condensation of language and attention to rhythm and line structure—I would say *yes*. However, my poems are narrative, often telling stories, so they're somewhat similar to my prose. I think my prose is lyrical, too.

AM: Who are the writers that have influenced you, and to which writer would you say you owe the greatest debt?

JND: My first response to this question is always D.H. Lawrence, mostly because of his novel *Sons and Lovers*, which was the first work of his that I read as a young teenager. At that time, I was moved by the romance, especially between Paul and Miriam, but now when I read it as an adult, it's obvious that the relationship between the son and his parents and the dynamics between Paul's parents are most compelling and what have affected me.

The English midlands setting of Lawrence's work, especially as described in *Sons and Lovers*, has always reminded me of my Western North Carolina landscape, particularly as it was in my childhood. Lawrence's boyhood coal mining village of Eastwood is reminiscent of the Clinchfield Cotton Mill village where my mother grew up.

As far as poetry goes, Dante Gabriel Rossetti's "Alas, So Long!" is a favorite, and Poe's "Annabel Lee," with its internal rhyme and alliteration—devices I use in my poems—has no doubt influenced me.

AM: Thank you, Julia, for taking the time to do this interview, and best of luck with everything.

JND: Thank you, Allen, for allowing me to share this information about *Barefoot in the Snow* and for giving me the opportunity to reflect upon my life as a poet.

Coleman Hutchison

AM: Thank you, Dr. Hutchison, for doing this interview, and congratulations on the publication of this fine book, *Apples and Ashes*.

You address this question at length in your book, but I'll ask the question anyway for the benefit of those who have not yet read *Apples and Ashes*. Why do you think your book is one of the first to comprehensively analyze Confederate literature and literary culture? Why out of the thousands of books about the Old South and the Civil War has there been no extensive literary history of the Confederacy?

CH: To my mind, there are three key reasons for the neglect of Confederate literature. The first is an assumption made by several generations of historians and literary critics: that there wasn't much of the stuff and in any case it wasn't very good. At first blush this assumption seems sound. Confederate writers and publishers were perpetually beleaguered. They faced severe shortages of paper, ink, type, skilled labor, and printing presses. Thus, it is with good reason that scholars would assume that Confederate literature was meager in both quantity and quality. Yet, as a number of bibliographies attest, and as my book makes clear, the Confederacy produced a startling array of literary texts. And even if a great deal of it proves to be so much patriotic bluster, such patriotic bluster is of great historical interest. After all, Confederate national feeling helped to bring about the most cataclysmic war in American history, one with more than 620,000 casualties.

Second, there is the problem of Confederate defeat. The Confederate States of America failed, and failed spectacularly. The Confederacy was, above all else, a short-lived and often chaotic experiment in nation building. Unfortunately, historians and literary critics have few models for thinking about such failed experiments, especially the emergence and collapse of a nation over the course of a mere fifty-one months. Perhaps more to the point, readers know how this story ends—at Appomattox, in defeat, as ashes—so why should they care about the *aspirations* of Confederate writers? My book asks us to return to a moment when both a Confederate nation and a Confederate national literature were real possibilities, not merely lost causes. Although it doesn't offer a counterfactual history—What would have happened if the Confederates had won the war?—it does emphasize Confederate literature's once-great expectations over its stultifying disappointments.

Finally, I think literary historians in particular have avoided the literature of the Confederacy because they worry about the politics of treating an overwhelmingly conservative, even reactionary set of texts that made the case for a proslavery, antidemocratic republic. Put simply, no one wants to write about the bad guys—especially if that writing will be interpreted as personal sympathy with, or an apologia for, the bad guys. For many, to write about the Confederate nation is to risk being seen as endorsing its right to exist. My colleagues in history seem to have addressed any such political qualms. Over the past 25 years historians like Drew Gilpin Faust, Gary Gallagher, Anne Sarah Rubin, Stephanie McCurry, and Michael T. Bernath have produced immensely helpful histories of the Confederacy, none of which are apologias. Now it's time for literary scholars to do the same.

AM: You make a point to say that you find "almost nothing that is admirable in the politics and culture of the Civil War South." Such a disclaimer seems necessary for anyone wishing to engage in scholarship on the Confederacy. Why is that? Let me put this another way. Scholars in other fields usually do not find it necessary to separate their views from the views of their subjects, since that separation is generally already understood by readers. Why is

your subject different?

CH: I thought long and hard about whether to include such a disclaimer. In the end, I decided that clarity and transparency were important, in no small part because I think my colleagues' fears about the politics of writing about the Confederacy are well-founded. Alas, many people assume that a book written about the Confederacy is probably (perhaps secretly?) sympathetic to the Confederacy. I included the disclaimer in the opening pages of *Apples and Ashes* in order to force my readers to acknowledge, as you say, the separation between my views and the views of my subjects. But it was also a way to address forthrightly and quickly the politics of writing about the Confederacy before moving on to the real work at hand.

As my tone here suggests, I have very little patience for such handwringing, which, as I suggest above, is one of the reasons Confederate literature has been largely ignored for nearly a century and a half. Over the past several years I've given talk after talk on Confederate literature. I cannot tell you how many times I've been complimented for giving a "gutsy" conference presentation or public lecture. But there shouldn't be anything "gutsy" about merely doing my job—that is, trying to capture and help my readers to understand the messiness and alterity of the nineteenth century. It's not "gutsy" to pay attention to an understudied and significant literature that rewards close reading; it's actually part of my job description. I've also had no small number of conversations that begin with the questions, "Really, why would you want to write about these people? Are you a southerner? Did your ancestors fight for the Confederacy?" My answer is always the same: "Those people are of intense historical interest. Nothing more, nothing less. Oh, and I'm from Portland, Oregon, for whatever that's worth."

All of this brings to mind something the late Jay Fliegelman said about the *Heath Anthology of American Literature*'s exclusion of pro-slavery discourses. (The *Heath*, which was hugely important in making available a multicultural American literary canon, included a number of abolitionist texts.) To ignore such discourses was, Fliegelman wrote, to "embarrassingly reproduce a cultural history of winners. The voices of reaction have to be encountered in all their complexity and not assumed to be self-evident or dismissed as too offensive" (Anthologizing the Situation of American Literature, *American Literature* 65 [1993]: 335). This quotation serves as an epigraph for *Apples and Ashes,* and it was a guiding principle in researching the book. As I wrote, I kept thinking how much we lose when we only tell the winner's story, when we dismiss any part of a rich and vexed literary history.

AM: My review does not say enough about Confederate identification with England, particularly in the literary context. Your book, however, is in a sense "comparative." It seeks in various ways to show how Southerners tried to create a national literature that was distinct from the literature of other regions. Do you think *Apples and Ashes* contributes to the discipline of comparative literature or to what is now being called transnational studies?

CH: I take that as a high compliment, Allen. I, too, think of the book as a comparative study. My methodology was heavily influenced by postcolonial theory, the comparative history of nationalisms, and the sociology of culture. As a result, I understand literary nationalism to be a relative and contingent phenomenon, a function of cross-cultural comparison. At the risk of putting too fine a point on it, literary nationalism happens when people distinguish their literature from the literature of other people.

As you suggest, this was particularly the case with Confederate writers, who were exceedingly anxious about the relationship between their nascent literary culture and that of the United States and England. Such anxiety requires, then, that my book constantly shuttle between the Confederate and United States of America; the book also makes a number of unexpected detours to places in Europe and Latin America.

Because *Apples and Ashes* identifies a number of specific mechanisms by which literary nationalism helped to engender the Confederate States of America, I hope that my book will help scholars and readers to better understand the relationship between literature and nationalism more broadly. Although my book doesn't offer a theory of literary nationalism per se, it does tout the usefulness of the Confederate example for thinking about the role of literature in the imagining of political communities.

Finally, while *Apples and Ashes* makes clear the international roots and routes of Confederate literature, it also puts some pressure on the new transnational studies. I acknowledge that the "transnational turn" has been exceedingly productive for literary and cultural studies; at the same time, I worry that it has turned us away prematurely from the study of nations and nationalism. While I applaud the desire to "think and feel beyond the nation"—to write, that is, postnational, transnational, hemispheric, and global literary histories—I think there's still a great deal of work to be done with and on the nation. For instance, despite decades of intensive study, we seem no closer to a full understanding of the relationship between literature and nationalism. A wide range of scholars agree that there is something fundamentally "literary" about the construction of nationality, but details remain vague.

AM: *Apples and Ashes* is somewhat groundbreaking in its approach to an understudied subject. Is there related work that needs to be done in this area, a gap in scholarship that still needs to be filled?

CH: *Apples and Ashes* does not aim to be comprehensive; it is an idiosyncratic rather than a definitive literary history of the Confederacy. As such, I sincerely hope that this will be the first of many literary historical engagements with Confederate literature. (Indeed, I wrote my endnotes with the work of future scholars in mind.) There is still a great deal of work to be done on pre-Confederate southern literary nationalism (the subject of Chapter One). I also unearthed an immense amount of Confederate popular poetry. Scholars of nineteenth-century American poetry would do very well to treat some of these fascinating and troubling poems—many of which, I hasten to add, are available online. Finally, I'd love to see more scholarship on the relationship between the bellum and postbellum literatures of the South. In what ways did the literature of the Confederacy influence the literature of Reconstruction, to say nothing of the literature of the so-called "Southern Renaissance"? As this suggests, I also hope that my book will help to draw attention back to the literature of nineteenth-century South more broadly. (Alas, much of southern studies—both old and "new"—continues to privilege the twentieth and twenty-first centuries.)

AM: Which author do you think was most important to the development of Confederate literary nationalism?

CH: This is a very difficult question, especially since my book argues for the importance of amateur and anonymous Confederate writers. Nonetheless, I think William Gilmore Simms's lifelong advocacy for a distinct and distinctive southern literature was crucially important to the ways Confederates thought about their nascent national literature. (In Chapter One, I discuss the following, apocryphal 1856 Southern Commercial Convention resolution: "*Resolved*, That there be a Southern Literature. *Resolved*, That William Gilmore Simms, L.L.D., be requested to write this literature.") For this reason, I'm particularly excited about the work of the Simms Initiatives at the University of South Carolina. If scholars and readers can have easier access to Simms's enormous corpus of texts, then perhaps we can better understand Confederate literary culture and its legacies.

I also think Augusta Jane Evans was a pivotal figure for Confederate literary nationalism. On the eve of the war, the author of *Beulah* (1859) was one of the South's rising literary stars. By 1867, with the publication of *St. Elmo*, she had become one of nineteenth-century America's bestselling novelists. In between Evans produced one of the few successful Confederate novels, *Macaria* (1864), wrote passionately about the future of southern literature, and even pushed the Confederate Congress to extend reciprocal international copyright to foreign authors. There is still much, much work to be done on this recalcitrant figure.

AM: Thanks again for taking the time. I hope that many of our readers will purchase this book and take seriously its compelling arguments.

Jeffrey Tucker

AM: Jeff, this interview is exciting for me. It's something of a reversal of the interview that we did together in January 2011. This time, I'm interviewing you. I'd like to start off by asking about your two recent books, *Bourbon for Breakfast* **and** *It's a Jetsons World***. Tell readers a little about both books.**

JT: Both books cover the unconventional side of private life as governed by the market and human volition. I guess you could say that this is my beat. I'm interested in the myriad ways in which the government's central plan—and there is such a thing—has distorted and changed our lives, and also interested in the ways we can get around this plan and still live fulfilling lives. I take it as a given that everything that government does is either useless or destructive or both. The government does a tremendous number of things, so this is a huge area. *Bourbon* is more focused on the rottenness of the state and its harm, while *Jetsons* is more the marvelous things that markets do for us. Neither subject gets the attention they deserve.

AM: These books are available for free online in PDF and EPUB formats. Explain why you've chosen to make your work freely and widely available.

JT: Every writer wants to be read, so it only makes sense for all writers to post their material. Of course publishers tend to intervene here with promises of royalties in exchange for which you become their slave for the rest of your life plus 70 years (that's when they dance on your grave). This is the essence of copyright. It is a bad deal for writers. Those who go along with it these days nearly always regret it later. If they actually earn royalties—and very few actually do—it is likely they would have earned more had the material not been withheld pending payment. The bestselling books of 2012—the *Hunger Games* series—are posted by pirates everywhere, even against publisher wishes. But, you know, this is starting to change. Publishers are gradually seeing the point to posting material online. Sadly, they aren't budging on the copyright issue, which is really pathetic. No libertarian should ever publish anything with any institution that is not willing to embrace a very liberal policy on reprints, and one that is likely enforceable such as Creative Commons Attribution. Meanwhile, the government is using copyright, a phony form of property rights, to step up its despotic control over the digital age. The situation is extremely dangerous. One hundred years from now, they will be laughing at our times and poking fun at how the anachronistic state tried its best to thwart progress.

AM: You strike me as an optimist. Is that true?

JT: Not as a matter of principle but there are certain rational reasons to be very hopeful about the future. The future is always uncertain except in this one sense: it will be different from today. The state is very bad at managing change. Freedom is very good at managing change. Freedom is a form of play, a relentless process of adaptation, trial and error, of testing and pushing out the boundaries. Freedom is really marvelous at implementing an infinite world of ideas, whereas the state pretty much has only one idea: push people around. This is why freedom always ends up outrunning the ability of the state to manage it. Freedom is smarter, and connects more closely with human ambitions and dreams, and this is especially true in a digital age. For this reason, I think we have reason to be full of confidence and hope.

AM: After a long tenure at the Ludwig Von Mises Institute, you recently became publisher and executive editor of Laissez Faire Books. A lot of people are anxious to see what you're going to do with that enterprise. What can you tell them at this point?

JT: Well, I'm glad to report that we are selling books and

that's fantastic. We also have some two dozen books in the process toward publication. I'm being pretty fussy with the books overall, commissioning excellent introductions and writing all sorts of editorial prefaces and things. As we approach summer, you will see many more wonderful things happen, things that have never been done before, but I think I'll let the details be a surprise.

AM: What is Laissez Faire Books? Many readers of this site are probably unfamiliar with it.

JT: The company has this brilliant history that traces to 1972. Murray Rothbard was in many ways at the center of its founding but there were also many Randians involved. Between that point and the digital age, it was the main way that people received libertarian literature. Oddly, one thing I've noticed since coming to work here is that the "curator" role is still something that Laissez Faire can play. If we can guarantee a certain number of sales on a particular book, we can make the difference as to whether it is published or not. Much to my surprise, this seems to be happening already.

I'm extremely pleased that Agora Financial took over LFB in 2011. Agora is a for-profit company with offices all over the world, and the firm has a dynamic ethos that embraces commerce, change, and progress. The past is just data in a company like this, while all the energy/action is in the future. As you might imagine, I like this environment. It is a natural home for me.

AM: Thank you so much for taking the time, Jeff. Is there anything else you'd like to say before we conclude?

JT: I have a strong sense these days that libertarianism, broadly considered, is undergoing huge changes in strategic outlook, and I'm happy about that. We are moving away from the "movement" mentality of the analog age and into a broader sense of the global universe of ideas. This means taking more risks, exploring more areas, and generally having more fun than ever. It's a good time to love liberty.

AM: Thank you so much. This was really great, and I hope we can do it again.

JOHN SHELTON REED

AM: Thank you for taking the time to do this interview, John. I know that readers of *Southern Literary Review* **are excited to hear from you.**

Dixie Bohemia **began, your Introduction explains, with the substance of the Fleming Lectures you delivered at Louisiana State University in April 2011. Here we are just a year and a half later, and the book is already printed, bound, and on bookshelves. How did you manage that?**

JSR: When I was invited to give the lectures, I had a choice: I could write the lectures and then turn them into a book, or write the book and extract the lectures. I had enough time to do the latter, so the year and a half after the lectures was spent tidying up, getting permission to use illustrations, and, of course, copy-editing, proof reading, and actual production.

AM: Of all of the famous "Creoles," which is your favorite?

JSR: So many of them were fascinating characters. . . . Probably Natalie Scott. She won the Croix de Guerre as a Red Cross nurse in World War I, then went back to New Orleans to be a first-rate reporter as well as a society columnist. She wrote a play and several cookbooks, rode her horse to Mexico, was active in the Junior League, made a lot of money investing in French Quarter real estate, knew everybody, and turned up everywhere. Later, she moved to Mexico and did a great many good works there, then re-upped with the Red Cross for World War II.

AM: I take it that few people, save for the specialists and

Faulkner aficionados, know a great deal about this part of Faulkner's history—that is, the New Orleans part, before he was really famous and while he was living with William Spratling. I, for one, was surprised by what I learned from reading your book. Do you think there is more work to be done on this portion of Faulkner's life?

JSR: I don't think there's really a lot of research left to do: Those specialists and aficionados have documented his life damn near day by day. I drew extensively on Joseph Blotner's huge biography, for instance. Anything that's not in that biography, or Joel Williamson's Faulkner book, or Kenneth Holditch's articles, or elsewhere in "the literature" probably can't be retrieved at this point. About all that can be done is to rearrange it and make it more accessible to the idly curious – which is pretty much what I tried to do.

AM: As a fan of John William Corrington, I had been more aware of the bohemian social spaces in New Orleans much later in the 20th century—these were ably detailed by Jeff Weddle in a similarly titled book, *Bohemian New Orleans*—but I was pleased and intrigued by your account of the Prohibition Era. At one point in your book, you ask the question "Why New Orleans?" I'd like to put that question to you here, even though the answer is, plain as day, in the book. You may object if you like—"Objection! Asked and answered!"—but I can't help but ask.

JSR: It's not an easy argument to summarize, but I listed a number of factors that made New Orleans the Southern city most hospitable to an emerging Bohemia. First of all, it had Tulane, which employed and produced artists, writers, architects, and anthropologists who were part of the scene. It had four intensely competitive newspapers that also provided income and employment, as well as publicizing the circle's activities and attracting new members. The city's Jewish community–large, by Southern standards—was deeply involved in the arts; it provided both resources and recruits. The same could certainly be said about the gay community. The French Quarter was picturesque, and cheap, and full of exotic Sicilians who supplied bootleg alcohol in quantity. Finally, the city's Bohemians shared an interest in historic preservation with older "Uptown" folks and a taste for les bon temps with younger ones; there was a sort of symbiotic relation between Bohemia and "Society" that I find hard to imagine in any other Southern town.

AM: What strikes me about your writing, here as elsewhere, is your ability to slip sociological insights into what would seem like entertaining history. You define "social circles," for instance, and you take great pains to relate unique cultural phenomena to a distinct geographical space, all the while showing how the culture and the place relate to, and effect, one another. Is this a result of your training as a sociologist? Do you make a concerted effort to avoid the academic, esoteric jargon that, in my opinion, plagues the writing of many intellectuals?

JSR: Thank you for noticing the sociology, but also for saying it's unobtrusive. As for its presence—I've been a practicing sociologist going on 50 years now, and I reckon I can't help it. I'd like to think it adds something to what would otherwise be just a bunch of good stories. (Not that there's a thing wrong with just telling good stories.) But I don't want to scare people off or bore them, so I don't pound the sociology into them. I hope they'll just absorb it. I do work at my writing because I want to reach readers other than the half-dozen sociologists who are interested in the same things I am. I also try hard to make it look easy. I recently learned the word "sprezzatura." That's what I want to achieve.

AM: Thank you so much for taking the time to answer these questions, John. You're always welcome here at *Southern Literary Review*.

WILLIAM BERNHARDT

AM: Thanks for doing this interview, Bill. You're a prolific author, having written dozens of books. Do you have a favorite among the books you've authored?

WB: I think *Primary Justice* will always have a special spot in my heart, because it was the first novel I wrote and the first that I sold, and of course, it was a big success that has now led to eighteen other books featuring lawyer Ben Kincaid. Creating that whole world from scratch, though, learning something new each day, was fun and exciting.

AM: Your latest book is *Justice Returns*. It's the latest installment in the Ben Kincaid series. When you began that series, did you think it would ever involve this many books?

WB: No, not remotely. I thought *Primary Justice* was a self-contained, character-driven novel, and even now, if you read it, it comes to a definitive conclusion, not a "Tune in next week." Stupid me. My editor at Random House/Ballantine, Joe Blades, saw potential in these characters that had never occurred to me. From the start, he said, "This should be a series. Let's do a three-book contract."

AM: You're a lawyer by training. Did you find the transition from legal writing to fiction writing to be natural or difficult?

WB: Writing is always difficult, but at least when writing the courtroom scenes, I had some experience and credibility I could bring to the table. Other subjects, like forensics and police procedure, I had to learn from scratch.

AM: You also write poetry.

WB: I have always loved and written poetry, but it took a while for me to work up the courage to publish it. I find it to be the most challenging form of writing, so it's only appropriate to have some experience before I even attempted it. Though my poetry is probably lower profile than my novels, it has inspired some of the best reviews I've had in my entire career.

AM: Who are your favorite poets?

WB: Today, Billy Collins and Tracy Smith. In the past, there are too many to choose from. Emily Dickinson. Wordsworth. Donne. That Shakespeare guy is pretty talented, too.

AM: You're a publisher as well as a writer. How did you get into publishing?

WB: To me, it's just part of being in the literary world, and specifically, giving back to a world that has been so kind to me. We have two imprints, Balkan Press, which focuses on poetry and literary fiction, and Babylon Books, which publishes popular fiction. We also publish a literary journal called *Conclave*.

AM: I'm always curious about how authors of thrillers develop suspenseful plots. Do you do it the same way for each of the Kincaid novels, or is each book approached differently? What are your methods?

WB: I'm not sure I have a method. Ideas start to accumulate. In my mind, I think about how to make many good ideas fit together into a larger plot. Eventually, I have enough to start writing.

AM: Did you ever receive formal training in creative writing, or did you just start writing one day?

WB: I've written since I was in grade school, and even wrote something I called a novel in the sixth grade. I did take some writing courses in college that were helpful. But of course, the best teacher is experience.

AM: What was it like when you found out your first book was getting published?

WB: A great day. For years, I'd heard people telling me I was dreaming, being unrealistic. And then suddenly a had a book with a major publishing house getting major front-list treatment. Validating, to say the least.

AM: Thanks for the interview, Bill. Looking forward to doing another one.

Acknowledgments

I would like to thank the following publications in which these interviews first appeared: *The American Spectator*, *The University Bookman*, *The Addendum* (a publication of the Alabama State Bar), *Prometheus Unbound*, and *Mises Wire*. Most of these interviews first appeared in *Southern Literary Review*, which I have had the privilege of editing since 2011. Some of these interviews appeared on my blog, *The Literary Lawyer*.

About the Author

Allen Mendenhall is associate dean at Thomas Goode Jones School of Law, executive director of the Blackstone & Burke Center for Law & Liberty, and editor of *Southern Literary Review*. Visit his website at AllenMendenhall.com.

www.ingramcontent.com/pod-product-compliance
Lightning Source LLC
Chambersburg PA
CBHW030317080526
44584CB00012B/593